Diane Cooksey I

Simple

Meditations
on Friendship
& Spirituality

Gift

Judson Press® Valley Forge

GOD'S SIMPLE GIFT: MEDITATIONS ON FRIENDSHIP AND SPIRITUALITY

Copyright © 1988
Judson Press, Valley Forge, PA 19482-0851

Unless otherwise indicated, Bible quotations in this volume are from the *New English Bible* (NEB). Copyright © The Delegates of the Oxford University Press and the Syndics of the Cambridge University Press, 1961, 1970.

Other quotations of the Bible are from

The Revised Standard Version of the Bible, copyrighted 1946, 1952 © 1971, 1973 by the Division of Christian Education of the National Council of the Churches of Christ in the U.S.A., and used by permission.

LIBRARY OF CONGRESS
Library of Congress Cataloging-in-Publication Data

Kessler, Diane Cooksey.
  God's simple gift : meditations on friendship and spirituality / by Diane Cooksey Kessler.
    p.   cm.
  ISBN 0-8170-1141-2
  1. Friendship—Meditations. I. Title.
BJ1533.F8K44 1988
241'.676—dc19   88-9059
                                                        CIP

The name JUDSON PRESS is registered as a trademark in the U.S. Patent Office.
Printed in the U.S.A.

This book is dedicated to

Susannah Baker

and

James Luther Adams

each of whom has taught me much
about the meaning of friendship.

Prayer

Almighty and most gracious God,
whose very nature is to be present in good times and in
    bad;
in warm days and in cold;
in wind, rain, and sunny life;
in laughter and in pain;
in joy and in despair;
in work and in play;
and in all those things that are a joy of life,
open our hearts and our minds to the realities of the
    present
here and now.

Turn back, O God, the outer layers of our selves,
and look beneath the surface to our hidden inner
depths.
Many of us hide behind polite dreams and wooden
    responses—
not daring to admit to others or even to ourselves
that we are vulnerable.
Yet we turn to you, trusting,
knowing that you will handle us carefully and tenderly.

Turn back the outer layers of apparent courage,
and find our fears.
Address them in us.
Acknowledge them,
even as you cause us to acknowledge them before you.

Do it not so much to rid us of them,
though we would like to be rid of them
and free from fears for ever.
How wonderful it would be
to stand in the presence of your perfect love
that casts out fear.

Turn back the outer layers of apparent confidence,
and find our worries and our anxieties.
Address them in us.
Acknowledge our uncertainties,
even as we acknowledge them before you.
Do it not so much to rid us of these fears and anxieties,
though we would like to walk along some waterway
and watch our worries and anxieties drown
in the backwash behind us.
How wonderful it would be
to stand in the presence of your perfect love
that calms fears, storms, and worries.
Still our plea would be more modest:
to know that you are present with us
and that we are not alone
in our struggle with worry.

Turn back the outer layers of apparent certainty,
and find our doubts.
Address them in us.
Help us to acknowledge doubts without shame.
Do it not to rid us of our doubts,
for we would not want to forfeit the growth
that comes from ourselves and our doubts,
even while we seek your purest presence.
So, O God, our plea is more modest:
to make our doubts building blocks
to a finer and firmer faith,
and to know that you accompany us in our journey.

We ask not that you make the hard moments of life easier,
except that our burdens are
eased by the assurance of your companionship,
heightened by the knowledge of your loving care,
strengthened by hope,
and shaped by love,
even as was the one in whose name we pray,
Jesus Christ,
our Lord and Savior.
Amen.

Arthur D. Gray, from the Twelfth General Synod, 1979, adapted. Reprinted from *Book of Worship* © 1986 by permission of the United Church of Christ Office for Church Life and Leadership.

Contents

Preface

I became interested in the subject of friendship and spirituality through my own experiences. I have been blessed by some good friends. I have found that over the years these relationships have not only deepened my understanding of the meaning of friendship but also enriched my understanding of God as friend.

When I began to explore the interplay between friendship and spirituality more intentionally, I found that the theme of God as friend recurs periodically throughout Christian history in a wide array of writings by saints (Protestant, Catholic, and Orthodox) and mystics. Yet most of the writing on the subject has been done by philosophers rather than theologians. The one notable exception is Aelred of Rievaulx's *Spiritual Friendship.* Aelred was a Cistercian abbot who died on January 12, 1167. Writing at a time when friendship among monastics was, for the most part, discouraged, Aelred raised a counter voice. Among twentieth-century contemporaries, most who write about friendship—even among the "religiously inclined"—do so primarily from a psychological perspective.

And so I began to explore the subject of friendship and spirituality in a series of sermons, the results of which (with minor modifications in all but Chapters 1 and 9) comprise this book.

The purpose of the book is to explore the relationship between human friendship and God as friend. This is not done in any systematic fashion. Rather, I invite the reader to join me on a journey which still is in process. The terrain has been visited many times before, but the frequency of exploration has not diminished the freshness of discovery. And, in the final analysis, each person's journey is uniquely his or her own. Each of us can add insights to the collective experiences of the ages.

This book was developed with several goals in mind:

1. to explore some theological implications in the human experiences of friendship as a way of fostering a fuller understanding of God;

2. to improve our human capacities to give and receive friendship, as part of the divine mandate for humanity;

3. to nurture our capacities to be open to God by drawing on a familiar aspect of human experience, namely, friendship;

4. to examine some implications of friendship as it impacts community (both church and world); and

5. to foster the capacity for spiritual nurture as part of a full friendship.

I have tried to use some of the rich resources from the Protestant spiritual traditions as illustrations. This has been an intentional effort. Too many of us are unfamiliar with this aspect of our own history. Yet our Protestant forebears have written a wealth of devotional literature, much of which could enliven our own spiritual pilgrimages if only we were aware of its existence. I hope that by my mentioning just a few of these "leading lights," some people will be spurred on to do a little exploration of their own in some of this literature.

This book has been designed for dual uses. It may serve as a source of personal meditation or small-group study and reflection. Some suggested questions for thought and discussion have been included in the Appendix to assist groups that want to explore this topic together. Bible readings and brief prayers relevant to each chapter have been offered for individuals who want to combine Bible study, meditation, and prayer.

At this point, I want to offer a word of explanation about the Scripture passages quoted in the text. They are taken either from the *New English Bible* (I appreciate the freshness of the translation) or the Revised Standard Version. I have sought to be gender inclusive by adding [in brackets] whenever such an addition is consistent with the meaning of the text. This sometimes reads awkwardly. Until we find a satisfactory resolution to the dilemmas concerning inclusive language, however, these infelicities are a small price to pay for the capacity to incorporate women comfortably into the reading and meanings in Scripture.

I owe special thanks to the Reverend Jean Curtis and the members of West Concord Union Church (United Church of Christ) in Concord, Massachusetts, who invited me to lead three Sunday morning seminars on this subject in the fall of 1985. Those good people gave me an opportunity to "test out" some of this material in a small-group context, and I found the experience enriching.

Thanks, also, to the friends and staff of the Massachusetts Council of Churches, with whom I have shared an ecumenical ministry these past twelve years. A three-month sabbatical, authorized by the MCC board of directors, enabled me to complete this project. These sermons have profited greatly from frequent comments, suggestions, and bibliographical references given by the Reverend Dr. James A. Nash, Executive Director. Administrative assistants Ms. Judith Lambert and Ms. Elizabeth Shippee have given patient and careful attention to the tasks of typing, first the sermons, then the manuscript.

This book is primarily for devotional use. I hope, however, that others more gifted than I will make a more systematic exploration of the theological implications of friendship and spirituality. All of us could benefit from such work.

Diane Cooksey Kessler
July 31, 1987

Section 1

Human Friendship As It Illumines the Divine

⟶≫ 1 ≪⟵

Simple Gifts

The nature of human *love* between friends, as evidenced in trust, loyalty, thoughtfulness, tolerance, forgiveness, and flexibility; the ways in which these dimensions of human love provide a glimpse of the nature of God's love; the place of the *incarnation* in making the connections.

Isaiah 9:6-7; John 15:12-17

Americans live in a fast-paced era of instants—instant coffee, instant replays, instant analyses. We depend on "now" bank accounts, fast food, rapid transits. Many of us feel overworked, overprogrammed, overstimulated. Or, if we happen to have retired from such frenzied activity and, because of health or circumstance, no longer are able to move at such a frantic pace, we may feel instantly marginalized.

In such an era, relationships—which take time, require

nurture, and demand attention—are in danger of getting lost or, at least, "put in their place" somewhere on the fringes of our existence. Many professional men and women have left such "expendables" behind in their search for career conquests. By the end of the day or week little energy is left for friendship.

At the same time, we recognize the need for friendship. Indeed, we long for intimacy. The popularity of computerized dating services, singles clubs, and other structured means of "getting people together" seems to confirm our human hunger.

But all too often, we want to short-circuit the process—to leap from acquaintance to intimacy, bypassing a probationary period which is the soil from whence any solid friendship gets nurtured and sustained. And then we feel disappointed, disillusioned, cheated somehow, when our hopes do not correspond with reality. These are some of the dilemmas of friendship formation in our contemporary society. So what does the real thing look like? If we were to restore friendship as a vocation worthy of our time and attention, what would the task require of us? What are some of the marks of authentic friendship?

Trust. A friend, in the words of the medieval Abbot Aelred, is someone "to whom we can fearlessly entrust our hearts." In other words, a friend is someone we can believe in and rely on, in whose presence we can be without fear or misgiving. We can simply *be,* without pretention.

Loyalty. "And they were friends. They were pals. They stuck together through thick and thin."[1] Such is the description of four characters in a popular children's story. Friends are faithful. They weather the storms of suffering, the temporary boredoms, the distances, and the disagreements.

Thoughtfulness. Friendship is nourished in the soil of unselfish concern, sensitivity, and kindness. It is bonded to-

---

[1] Crosby Bonsall, *The Case of the Dumb Bells* (New York: Harper & Row, Publishers, Inc., 1982), p. 8.

gether by years of little gestures—the yearly Valentine's Day card sent to your child who loves to receive mail but rarely does; the spontaneous phone call "just to check up on how you're doing"; the special attention during times of stress or bereavement.

Tolerance. If we examine the evidence of creation, we are forced to conclude that God not only permits but appears to revel in diversity. A mark of friendship is the capacity, at worst, to allow this diversity and, at best, to celebrate our respective idiosyncracies.

Forgiveness. As God sets us free from the consequences of our own acts of alienation, so we are called to free each other. Few sustained friendships can escape the trauma of occasional disagreements and insensitivities. Friendship can not maintain itself without the resiliency which is born of genuine forgiveness.

Flexibility. Friendship is non-possessive. It has a way of spilling out beyond itself. It does not constrict. It enhances.

These, then, are some of the marks of authentic human friendship. This is what it looks like. It is a simple gift. It also is a blessing of God. In fact, it can illumine our relationship with God. And friendship—both with God and humanity—is within reach of everyone.

How many of us are blessed with this simple gift? How many of us could be better givers? Where does this dimension of life rank in our order of priorities—in the way we use our time? What bearing can it have on our religious life—our understanding of God? These questions are worth pondering.

One of the discoveries I have made is that it is much easier to understand all the religious talk about the love of God if it has a "skin face." The Gospel of John asserts that being a friend of God involves being friends to each other—"loving one another." The two are intimately related.

One of the ways in which we can grow to understand the love of God is through the experience of receiving *and giving* human love. One context in which we can know this fully and clearly is in human friendship. Friendship certainly is not the only ingredient in a full Christian life. But it is one essential ingredient.

Jesus says that we may claim the title "friends of God" to the degree that we take seriously the vocation of human friendship. In asserting this, he poses a challenge to each one of us.

This is one key message of the incarnation. Each year during the season of Advent, when we anticipate the birth of Christ, I find myself focusing on what God might be saying to us through Mary's firstborn. And I am repeatedly struck by the *ordinariness of the incarnation.* I continue to marvel at it. Just think! This glimpse of God was born in a barn, a helpless infant like any other babe in swaddling clothes, arriving—as babies often do—unexpectedly, placed in a makeshift manger. It was a gift born in love—so very common, but also so very much like God.

This focus on the extraordinary ordinariness of God revealed in human flesh catches us by surprise. We are so used to hearing the story of Christ's birth amidst centuries of accumulated Christian pageantry that we have lost the point. God is revealed primarily in simple human encounters where love is made manifest.

What we know of God, through Jesus Christ, should inform our ordinary human relationships. What we experience in these ordinary human encounters potentially may enrich and enliven our understanding of God. In this way, *all* of life matters, in its everydayness as well as its crisis-times, its communal as well as its interpersonal dimensions.

Indeed, this simple gift of our everyday lives—the gift of friendship—reveals important insights about God, about ourselves, and about our human relationships. This is one key message of the incarnation. That simple Babe in swaddling clothes brings to us a simple gift of profound proportions—the gift of human love. God seems to be saying to us, "See. Here I am, right under your nose, so obvious that you will trip over Me if you're not careful. You will find Me in the humility of a stable, in the weakness of an infant, in the wonder of new life, in love like that evoked by a babe. You will find Me in the ordinary things of life. You will get a glimpse of Me through friendship."

Love is the litmus test. Human encounters are the living and learning laboratory. And the life of the Spirit is enhanced as we engage in the gift of life with others.

Let us examine this simple gift even further. Recall some of the qualities that are marks of human friendship: trust, loyalty, thoughtfulness, tolerance, forgiveness, flexibility. In each case, are not these also qualities of God, as the church has led us to perceive the divine through its encounter with the incarnate Christ?

We certainly confess this to be the case through our hymn singing: "A mighty fortress is our God, a bulwark never failing." God, we confess through hymn singing, is the ultimate being to whom we can fearlessly entrust our hearts. "O love that wilt not let me go, I rest my weary soul in thee." God is faithful. Even when we cannot hold on any longer, the love of God will not let us go. "All that we have is thine alone, a trust, O Lord, from thee." God is the ultimate source, the ultimate giver. "In Christ there is no east or west, in him no south or north!" In God we celebrate our global diversity, unified through love. "Judge not the Lord by feeble sense, But trust him for his grace." The forgiving graciousness of God, freely given, is the context in which we imperfect creatures live and love. "Immortal Love, forever full, Forever flowing free, Forever shared, forever whole, A never-ebbing sea!" God's love is boundless. It moves where it will, given to those whom we least expect, under circumstances we cannot predict, with a compassion we cannot control. It frees us to love each other.

What we know of God through Christ should inform our ordinary human relationships. We are called to bring loving qualities such as trust, loyalty, thoughtfulness, tolerance, forgiveness, and flexibility into all that happens between friends, to say nothing of parent and child, husband and wife, indeed, ideally of all human encounters.

Friendship is a simple gift. It is a space in our lives where we can breathe deeply the fresh air of loving acceptance, where we can experience the joy of receiving though giving, in a world that often is too much with us in its ragged ambiguities and its tragedies.

Although I have focused so far on only one aspect of friendship, the interpersonal, my ecumenical commitments and institutional predilections lead me to ask if friendship has implications beyond itself, in the communal aspects of our lives. The answer to this question is a clear, strong yes.

Let me give some examples. A few years ago, for the first time after I had spent nearly a decade working in a council of churches, a meeting of clergy and administrative leaders in state government was co-sponsored by separate Protestant and Roman Catholic organizations in the state. The purpose of the meeting was to express our common hopes and concerns about the needs of welfare recipients. The unified concern of the churches enhanced the power of our presentation. This common effort among Protestants and Catholics was a significant sign of a key aim of the ecumenical movement—to make visible our Christian unity, for the sake of the world.

This jointly sponsored meeting probably would not have occurred, however, without years of gradually increasing contact by the staff in both institutions. Without the carefully cultivated trust, sensitivity, tolerance, forgiveness, and flexibility nurtured through years of phone consultations, luncheon conversations, and post-meeting socializing, that ecumenical effort might never have occurred.

When I scan the history of the churches, I am struck by how significant this "friendship factor" has been in achieving ecumenical breakthroughs. Visions of church unity finally embodied in the United Church of South India began a century before, as missionaries began to communicate and share. The director of the Baptist Mission Press in Calcutta, for example, took the simple, but previously untried, step of inviting his denominational colleagues to breakfast periodically. That seemingly small step began a movement of love and cooperation from which future generations were able to reap the benefits.

The merger of the Congregational Christian churches and the Evangelical and Reformed churches to form the United Church of Christ was over thirty years in the making. The union might not have occurred without the sustained friendship and shared vision of a handful of religious leaders who stuck together through thick and thin, undergirded by their common faith and nourished by their Christian friendship.

Friendship, then, has a life of its own, occasionally larger than the individuals involved. And here, too, "God is working God's purpose out," as one of my favorite hymns confesses.

One of the beauties of these ecumenical friendships, simultaneously threatening, is that bridges of the heart are built among people who, in many ways, really are very different. Human nature being what it is, we tend to seek out those who feel familiar, because they are mirror images of ourselves. But many of the rich and exciting discoveries about life can be made as we are willing to break out of the familiar, to reach beyond the accustomed, to move into the unexpected.

When we ponder the extraordinary ordinariness of the incarnation, it draws us to God who is revealed in an unexpected, yet simple human encounter with Mary's firstborn. It is a simple gift, born in love. We glimpse this gift, centuries old, fresh as today, as we live it out with each other in friendship.

PRAYER ⟪⟪⟫

Dear God, You have revealed Yourself through the profoundly simple gift of Jesus Christ; You have come to me in love, as my Friend; You appear to me wherever this love is manifested among friends. I can only respond in gratitude for this gift of grace. Help me to break out of the familiar, to reach beyond the accustomed, to move into the unexpected, to persist in giving the gift of friendship. And let me see Your face whenever this gift is received and nurtured. Amen.

→》》 2 《《←
What's Your Theme Song?

The nature of *forgiveness* between friends; the way in which this experience can lead us to ponder the nature of divine/human relations, since forgiveness in Christ is the primary point of encounter between fallen humanity and a forgiving God; what this means in understanding *salvation* by grace through faith.

Hosea 11:1-4, 8-9; Matthew 9:9-13

I Love You Just the Way You Are" is the title of a tune that was popular a few years ago. It has become a theme song for Dolores Hope, who sings it to husband Bob, and us, near the close of his TV "specials." I always get sentimental at that point. If she really means it, after all those years of marriage, she is singing volumes about that relationship. For no marriage, no family, no institutional relationship, no friendship can be sustained through the foibles and frailties of living without a healthy dose of forgiveness.

One qualification is necessary. Not all forms of behavior should be endured; not all kinds of hurt can be tolerated without doing serious harm to our psyches and our integrity. Forgiveness, however, is called for in all circumstances, regardless of the outcome. The Four Gospels maintain this ideal and demonstrate its practice on nearly every page. Forgiveness is part of responsible Christian living.

Unless we live hermetic lives, totally isolated from other people, we will have experiences—a lot of experiences—which test and stretch our capacities to forgive and to seek forgiveness. Without this capacity, friendships become brittle, shallow. With it, they can endure and evolve. Through it we can glimpse the nature of God's forgiving love.

Jesus often used human encounters to make a point about what God is like and how God expects us to behave. He was doing just that in the customhouse when he called Matthew to be his disciple. From what follows, we know that this, in itself, must have been scandalous.

As a tax-gatherer, Matthew collected revenues from the Palestinians for their heathen Roman conquerors. It was customary for tax collectors to squeeze as much money as they could from the people so they could keep a large margin of the profit for themselves. They were ingenious in their techniques. They put up toll gates on roads, bridges, and harbors. They charged duty on goods destined for market. They levied taxes on many common necessities, like salt. It is no wonder that they were despised. Just imagine the people's puzzlement when Jesus singled out one of these creatures to be a disciple!

To drive home his point, Jesus lingered among what Matthew's Gospel calls "many bad characters—tax-gatherers and others . . ." (9:10). When questioned about this behavior (as I suspect he knew he would be), he uttered three short sentences that point beyond the customhouse to a forgiving God: "It is not the healthy that need a doctor, but the sick. Go and learn what that text means, 'I require mercy, not sacrifice.' I did not come to invite virtuous people, but sinners" (vv. 12-13).

What is going on here? Our normal human expectations are being challenged, overturned, reversed. We expect Jesus to go after the "good guys," right? It fits with our concept of fairness. But he calls this concept into question: "It is not the healthy that need a doctor, but the sick. . . . I did not come to invite virtuous people, but sinners."

Jesus self-consciously was showing us, again and again, what God is like. And at this point, it appears that God is, indeed, the "Holy Other." Human beings tend to think of reward and punishment, "just deserts," and "turnabout as fair play." God, however, appears to respond in compassionate love.

In the Old Testament, God (through the prophet Hosea) describes the waywardness of a people and the forgiving love of the parent-God.

> When Israel was a boy, I loved him;
> I called my son out of Egypt;
> but the more I called, the further they went from me.
> —Hosea 11:1-2a

Then we hear God's anguished conclusion:

> How can I give you up, Ephraim,
> how surrender you, Israel? . . .
> My heart is changed within me,
> my remorse kindles already.
> I will not let loose my fury . . .
> for I am God and not a man [human],
> the Holy One in your midst.
> —Hosea 11:8-9

Israel was doing all sorts of bad things. God did not ignore the behavior. God was well aware of its outrageous, scandalous quality. God chose to reach out in love, despite the destructive distance of God's people.

We have here two examples—one from the Old Testament, another from the New, one of a whole nation, the other of an individual—of when human beings behave badly and they do not "get what they deserve" in the divine scheme.

We seem to have bumped into a paradox. God *is not* like us. God does not "play fair." God forgives the unforgivable, loves the unlovable. God does it here, now, fully, all at once. And yet, God *is* like us. As God forgives you and me, we are called to forgive each other. When we do this, we give each other a remarkable gift. We give each other a glimpse of the forgiving love of God.

So there you have it. When we apply this information to other people, it offends our sense of morality. When we apply the information to ourselves, we can not quite believe it.

Some of us deny that we live in a state of sin and brokenness which calls for forgiveness. As *Boston Globe* columnist Ellen Goodman said recently, "To err may be human, but to admit it has gone hopelessly out of date."[1]

Others remain bogged down in guilt, stuck in self-recrimination. To figure out if either applies to you, think for a minute about what goes on in your mind when you are sitting in church while the congregation corporately confesses its sins and then hears that we are forgiven. Do you tick off the items in the prayer and think, "Whew! That doesn't apply to me!" Or does your mind balk as the minister or priest proclaims the forgiveness of sins?

Either way, we miss the three-pronged message of the gospel on forgiveness.

1. No excuses can be offered for our brokenness as individuals and as communities. God requires the pure, hard truth. All of us, all of our churches, all of our societies have some mixture of strengths and weaknesses, virtues and vices, triumphs and failures. They are part of our identity. We should not complacently accept them. Nor, in all probability, can we completely eradicate them.

2. As the ethicist Paul Lehman observes,

God neither forgives us a little bit yesterday and a little bit more today, and still more tomorrow, nor does He forgive us for some things we have done while remaining displeased with others. God either forgives us here and now altogether,

[1]Ellen Goodman, "Forget the Fifth Amendment, I'm confessing," in *The Boston Globe*, Dec. 30, 1986, p. 19.

or He does not forgive us at all. That we are forgiven now
—this is the possession of that grace which is sufficient for
us.[2]

The Christian faith proclaims that we are forgiven *now,*
when we hear the Word, when we eat the bread, when we
take the cup.

3. Lehman also says,

> Forgiveness means that good people are as guilty as bad
> people, and bad people are as accessible to God as good
> people; and if good people object to so divine a dispensation,
> it only convicts them of aspiring to monopolize the grace of
> God which is the essence of hypocrisy.[3]

We come, then, to the heart of the matter. How do you
and I live our lives, in light of this Good News about God's
forgiving love? It is an appropriate question to ponder as we
consider the nature of friendship.

The response involves a twofold task: appropriating the
forgiveness which is ours through God in Christ and mirror-
ing this forgiveness among our friends and in the world.
Some remarkable things can happen when we live out of the
Good News of God's forgiving love.

Let me share with you one example. A few years ago in
a small Indiana town, some boys thoughtlessly lobbed a rock
at a passing Amish buggy. This wasn't the first instance of
"Amish-baiting," but it had the most serious consequences.
The stone struck a baby, Adeline Schwartz, and she died in
her mother's arms.

The youths were charged with reckless homicide—a crime
which could have led to several years in prison. But at the
trial an Amish bishop appealed for leniency. "The baby is
dead," he said. "Sending the men to prison won't bring it
back and the young men have suffered enough."[4]

The judge paid attention to this remarkable statement.

[2]Paul Lehman, *Forgiveness: Decisive Issue in Protestant Thought* (New York: Harper &
Row, Publishers, Inc., 1940), p. 139.
[3]*Ibid.,* p. 146.
[4]*Liberty,* vol. 81, no. 5 (Sept.-Oct. 1, 1986), p. 23.

Instead of sentencing the young men to prison, he fined them a substantial sum and ordered them to cover the family's costs for medical and funeral expenses. Since then, the youths reportedly have become "model citizens."

A tragic incident, which could have hardened the rancor between the Amish and their neighbors, instead evoked a new spirit of openness. An outside observer has noted that "Amish buggies . . . seldom draw more than a cheery wave from passing vehicles. Levi and Rebecca Schwartz like to think that each wave is a tribute to Baby Adeline."[5]

Forgiveness may not always be easy. In fact, it usually is not. But forgiveness is part of responsible Christian living. It is God's gift to us. It can be our gift to others.

So what's your theme song? Can you join Dolores Hope in singing "I love you just the way you are"? Now is as good a time as any to make a choice and live it out.

PRAYER

Gracious God, You have promised forgiveness to all who come to You with repentant hearts. I open my heart to You in all honesty and place the plain, hard truth of my brokenness in Your reconciling presence. Help me to experience the wholeness of Your healing love and to radiate this forgiveness in my friendships and in the world.
Amen.

[5]*Ibid.*

Section 2

The Significance of Some Ingredients in Human Friendship and Their Roles in Facilitating Our Openness to God

⇶ 3 ⇷

Humor: A Herald of Humility

The importance of *humor* as an integral part of religious life—its relationship to *humility*, its capacity to strengthen friendships, its significance as a bearer of God's blessings.

Isaiah 44:9-17; Matthew 6:1-18

I am a great fan of movies from the forties and fifties. In fact, I am a pushover for anything starring Van Johnson or Ray Milland. Among my favorites, however, is that Bing Crosby masterpiece of lyric sentimentality, *Going My Way.* In this film, Crosby plays the engaging "priest next door," as comfortable on a baseball diamond as at the altar rail. I have concluded that I like this Hollywood priest because he breaks apart my inherited, still harbored notions of piety as intense, boring, and humorless.

I suspect I am not alone in holding these assumptions.

Since religion deals with serious matters like "sin, death, and other unpleasant facts," we should not be surprised if our idea of "being religious" is skewed toward the sober. But outright slanted it is, if our understanding of piety is not broad enough to encompass the full range of human emotions, including humor. And so I want to make a plea for humor as a gift of God, a vital element in sustaining friendship, and an essential ingredient in a fully developed spiritual life.

The kind of humor I am talking about emerges from a kindly appreciation of life's incongruities. It can evoke anything from a quiet chuckle to a tearful belly laugh (the state to which I am reduced when Bill Cosby does his "visit to the dentist" routine). But the source is devoid of anger or cruelty. Rather, such humor celebrates life in, sometimes despite, all its subtlety and ambiguity.

What gives humor its delicious capacities? Good humor arises partly from *punctured pretentions*—a willingness to see life as it really is, unadorned by the veneer of vanity.

Mark Twain recognized this. One of my favorite Twain pieces is called a "Letter to the Earth."[1] This letter is addressed to one Abner Scofield, coal dealer, from a celestial source—the "Office of the Recording Angel"—who, according to Twain, is in charge of all prayer requests. In the letter the Recording Angel describes two kinds of prayers: (1) "Public Prayers, in which classification we place prayers uttered in Prayer Meeting, Sunday School, Class Meeting, Family Worship, etc."; and (2) "Secret Supplications of the Heart." The Recording Angel does not take "Public Prayers" as seriously as "Secret Supplications." The latter take precedence when discrepancies arise.

Abner Scofield's prayers were filled with discrepancies—inconsistencies between his public prayers and his private desires—duly noted and recorded by the Angel. My favorite

[1]Mark Twain, *Letters from the Earth* (New York: Harper & Row, Publishers, Inc., 1962), pp. 103-107.

is Secret Supplication no. 6, in which Abner prays for some form of violent death to a neighbor who had thrown a brick at the family cat while the cat was "serenading." This situation, the Recording Angel reports, conflicted with a Public Prayer of Scofield's that God should "be mercifully inclined toward all who would do us offense in our persons or our property." The Recording Angel suggests a modification in one or the other prayer, "to reconcile [the] discrepancy."

Twain zeroes in on a tendency in all of us to posture occasionally. We sometimes harbor distorted visions of ourselves (often inflated). We tend to see ourselves, others, and life in general as we think it should be rather than as it is. Twain humors us into *humility.*

A major temptation in life, to which clergy and other public figures may be especially (though not uniquely) prone, is to "play to the crowd." Jesus warned us about this, saying, "Beware of practicing your piety before men [people] in order to be seen by them" (Matthew 6:1, RSV). All of us are tempted to appear wiser, richer, purer, stronger than life—because we seek affirmation from the world, because we are afraid to acknowledge ourselves to ourselves, or because we are reluctant to reveal ourselves to God.

But God calls us to authenticity, to an open, realistic appraisal of our deepest intentions and of our own brokenness. The capacity to laugh at our shortcomings is one sign of authenticity. Humor, then, may be a herald of humility.

Good humor also arises from the *unmasking of idolatries.* It helps us to reorder our priorities, placing God at the top of the list. For example, the prophet Isaiah uses humor to point out the absurdity of Israelite idol worship. He simply describes the facts, and in so doing, we are humored into seeing the truth. The carpenter, Isaiah says,

> cuts down cedars; or he chooses a holm tree or an oak and lets it grow strong among the trees of the forest; he plants a cedar and the rain nourishes it. Then it becomes fuel for a man; he takes a part of it and warms himself, he kindles a fire and bakes bread; also he makes a god and worships it,

he makes it a graven image and falls down before it. Half of it he burns in the fire; over the half he eats flesh, he roasts meat and is satisfied; also he warms himself and says, "Aha, I am warm, I have seen the fire!" And the rest of it he makes into a god, his idol; and falls down to it and worships it; he prays to it and says, "Deliver me, for thou art my god!" (Isaiah 44: 14-17, RSV).

Isaiah uses satirical humor to show how silly it is for the Israelites to show devotion to a mere stick of wood.

Contemporary comedians potentially serve a prophetic role as well whenever they expose the idols we worship today—idols of wealth, success, fame, beauty, or tradition. I am a collector of religious and political cartoons. I have an office bulletin board filled with yellowing newspaper clippings in which assorted cartoonists have used humor to correct our political and religious vision.

I clipped one from *The American Baptist* magazine recently, depicting a modern man and a woman in old-fashioned stocks (the kind commonly used for punishment in the seventeenth century), as part of an exhibit labeled "Experiencing Our Baptist Heritage." The man is commenting, "If I had known *this* was our heritage, I wouldn't have been so *enthusiastic* about this idea!"[2] So much for an idolatrous, uncritical veneration of our religious traditions!

Humor, then, has a revelatory aspect. It punctures our pretentions and unmasks our idolatries.

Humor also is beneficent. It sometimes reveals surprising gifts. Two come immediately to mind.

First, our ties with friends, colleagues, indeed, the whole human family are strengthened through the shared laughter which comes from an unadorned recognition of our common lot and the sheer exuberance of life as a gift. What happens when we hear a good joke? We want to tell someone else, to share it. It is a simple, common human reaction.

Furthermore, the underlying possibilities for reconciliation and redemption give these simple acts a profound po-

[2]*The American Baptist,* May, 1984, p. 14.

tential. I think, for example, of Abraham Lincoln, famous for his "down-home" humor. Lincoln served this nation during one of its most perilous periods. Cabinet meetings often were tense affairs. Just when their strategic wrangling appeared to be reaching a flash point, Lincoln reportedly would interject a humorous anecdote and save the situation. Humor is potentially redemptive.

Second, in the process of learning humility through humor, we find God—forgiving, healing, loving "us most gently in the course of time."[3] The fourteenth-century English mystic Julian of Norwich experienced this sense of God's grace. She describes it as follows: "And here I understood that the Lord looked on the servant with pity and not with blame," Julian wrote, "for this passing life does not require us to live wholly without sin. He loves us endlessly, and we sin customarily, and he reveals it to us most gently."[4]

The Good News of the gospel is far better than many of us allow ourselves to believe. We profess the Protestant principle of justification by grace through faith, yet many of us still cannot quite believe it. The God we know in Jesus Christ is more interested in repentant reality than in pretentious piety. If we really believe this Good News, our joy in God's healing, forgiving love occasionally will well up inside us, and we will feel free to laugh—at ourselves, at our culture, and, yes, even at our churches!

Christianity is a religion of joy in the potential of God's creation and hope in the ultimate victory of life over sin and death. Christians are not blind to the tragedies in life or naive about the evil in our world. But we are saved from the abyss of despair by our faith, borne in the Christ event, nurtured in the church, sustained in our spirituality, attested to in our human relationships.

So we are allowed to laugh as we live out our faith. In fact, humor is essential. That which heals and saves is, of its

---

[3]Julian of Norwich, *Showings* (New York: Paulist Press, 1978), p. 304.
[4]*Ibid.*, p. 338.

nature, blessed by God. And humor is one of God's richest blessings.

PRAYER ⟪⟪⟪

Creator God, Who surprises us with the graceful gift of humor, help me to savor this good gift whenever I find it, as a sign of Your goodness. Use it to unmask my idolatries. Humor me into humility. And strengthen my bonds with others through laughter which is shared. In the name of Jesus Christ I pray.
Amen.

⇢⟫ 4 ⟪⇠
Time to Spare

The place of *play* in authentic, spiritually grounded Christian living—its relationship to *self-knowledge,* its importance in fostering the gift of friendship, its capacity to facilitate a *radical openness* to God.

Ecclesiastes 2:20-26

Christians at play. Is there a connection between religion and recreation? At first glance, we might say no. After all, religion is serious stuff, right? What does God have to do with the golf course—unless we mess up a perfect shot and take the Lord's name in vain?

But think again: about the wonder felt at the breathtaking beauty of some quiet corner of the coast; about the love shared with friends or family during a weekend "getaway"; about the exhilaration known at the successful completion of an arduous hike, a difficult sonata, a problematic putt.

Maybe there is more of a connection than we first imagined. Perhaps God is known not only in the serious side of life but also in the playful. But I am going to push even further. I believe that, under ordinary circumstances, we cannot know the gracious love of God in all its fullness without including recreation in the rhythm of our lives. Furthermore, we cannot know *ourselves* fully, as God sees us, unless we balance work and play. It follows, then, that recreation is as important as vocation in authentic, spiritually grounded Christian living. Is there a connection between religion and recreation? Absolutely.

Ecclesiastes understood the connection well. Unfortunately, Ecclesiastes may be one of the more neglected books in the Bible because his raw analysis of life is disturbing.[1] Ecclesiastes does not shrink from life's harsh realities. He begins his theological reflections by taking a hard-nosed look at life as he experiences it.

And what does he see? "A lonely man without a friend, without son or brother, toiling endlessly yet never satisfied with his wealth . . ." (4:8); a rich man (or woman) who "owns too much and cannot sleep" (5:12); righteous people perishing, wicked people prospering (7:15). Does it sound familiar?

Ecclesiastes' observations have a contemporary ring. Today's newspapers, magazines, and books are filled with "pop" psychological advice on combating the ills of our age. We still ask, "Why do bad things happen to good people?" (A Massachusetts rabbi has made a mint trying again to answer the question.[2]) We still bump into the brutal realization of our finitude. My dad says he daily scans the obituary column in his hometown newspaper and is relieved to see that his name is not listed. As Ecclesiastes observed, "There is nothing new under the sun" (1:9, RSV).

But Ecclesiastes does not stop with analysis. He also offers some answers—some solid theological insights—for the ills of the ages. The special value of this book is what the author *does* with his data. Ecclesiastes' reflections about life lived within the sacred space of God's grace lead to some conclusions we need to hear. The conclusions push us to see *play* as an integral part of Christian living.

Hear again the conclusions Ecclesiastes draws:

> There is nothing better for a man [or woman] to do than to eat and drink and enjoy himself [or herself] in return for his [or her] labours. And yet I saw that this comes from the hand of God. For without him [God] who can enjoy his [or her]

---

[1]The book's subtitle is "The Preacher." Hence, in our study we will refer to Ecclesiastes as a person.

[2]Harold S. Kushner, *When Bad Things Happen to Good People* (New York: Schocken Books, 1981).

34

food, or who can be anxious? God gives wisdom and knowledge and joy to the man [or woman] who pleases him [God],
while to the sinner is given the trouble of gathering and
amassing wealth only to hand it over to someone else who
pleases God. This too is emptiness and chasing the wind
(2:24-26).

This is *not* happy hedonism: eat, drink, and be merry, for
tomorrow we die. It *is* an appeal for *balance.* We are called to
"eat and drink" (in moderation, I am sure) and enjoy ourselves and our friends *in return* for our labor. And why are
we to live this way? Because all this—vocation and recreation—"comes from the hand of God."

Life is both gift and task. Its meaning is derived from the
gracious Giver. When we live life in the context of the Holy,
spurred by God's guiding will, sustained by God's forgiving
love, we receive "wisdom and knowledge and joy." Without
this context, life lacks durable meaning, and we find ourselves obsessed with "the trouble of gathering and amassing
wealth" or some other equally fruitless enterprise.

Ecclesiastes felt so strongly about this bit of wisdom that
he repeated it no less than five times throughout the book
(2:24-26; 3:12-15; 5:18-20; 8:15; 9:7). He reaches this conclusion through some solid theological reasoning.

Although we know enough of God's love to sustain and
guide, much of life remains shrouded in mystery. As Ecclesiastes says, "Whatever has happened lies beyond our grasp,
deep down, deeper than [we] can fathom" (7:24). Thus, we
have many unanswered questions, all signs of our humanity.
We are not God. We may wish we were, but we are not.

Not only do we lack divine wisdom, but we also lack
divine perfection! "The world contains no man [or woman]
so righteous that he [or she] can do right always and never
do wrong," Ecclesiastes observes (7:20). Centuries later,
Martin Luther reached the same conclusion after years of
scrupulous soul-searching in monkish seclusion. We cannot
"save ourselves" by striving for perfection. We will not
make it.

So the Reformer Martin Luther reached the same conclusion the Preacher Ecclesiastes had grasped centuries earlier:
"I know that it will be well with those who fear God" (8:12),
not in the simplistic sense of "live well and you'll be re-
warded." Rather, both discovered the gracious, giving, forgiving love of God, reflected in the ordinary gifts of life,
received only through faith in the Giver.

So what does all this religion have to do with recreation?
Play is grounded in a radical openness to God. When we
spend time in recreation, we give ourselves and God the
room to restore a right perspective on the meaning of life.
Play is one appropriate response to the Creator God's good
gift of creation. Play celebrates the gift and appreciates the
Giver.

We see clearly the connection between gift and giver
when both are human. How do you respond when your
four-year-old brings you an unexpected bouquet of wild
flowers? How do you feel when your spouse throws a surprise party to mark your fiftieth birthday? How do you react
when a friend spontaneously appears with a book "you just
have to read"? You respond with joy and gratitude.

So it should be in our response to God. As God loves us,
so we love ourselves, through our playful acts of re-creation,
and thus we are better able to love each other and God in
return.

Often, however, we have trouble, because the connections between God and humanity seem remote. Thus, we
tend to make three errors, which Ecclesiastes noted:

1. *We tend to place performance before people.* We get so caught
up in our work—whether it be earning a living, household
tasks, or even volunteer commitments—that the love of God
we might experience and give in "playtime" gets lost in our
activity and our exhaustion.

One of the best ways we can comprehend the love of God
is through love "of neighbor." God's Word of love was made
flesh and dwelt among us to *remove* some of the divine dis-

tance. In the life of Jesus, his contemporaries could *experience* God's love. It was tangible. They could see it. They could touch it. They could hug it!

This experience, however, was not unique. The *Spirit* of the experience, which we call "Holy," still dwells among us. We recognize it whenever we see love freely shared, given in the service of others, received in the Spirit in which it is given. All of this, however, requires awareness and takes time.

When we place performance before people, we short-change ourselves and others of opportunities to know and show the love of God.

A popular song during the Depression was called "Buddy, Can You Spare a Dime?" In the 1980s, when our lives are carefully compartmentalized into calculated responsibilities of defined duration, a new song is in order: "Sister, Can You Spare the Time?"

In our fast-paced era we are forced to be *intentional* about time. In order to "take time"—to savor the giftedness of life in fun, friends, and family—we must "make time."

2. A second *misperception* we often hold, clouding our capacity to play, is to see *wealth as a sign of worth.* Ecclesiastes honed in on this human foible. "I considered all toil and all achievement and saw that it comes from rivalry" between people (4:4). Then he makes the following observation: "Better one hand full and peace of mind, than both fists full and toil that is chasing the wind" (4:6).

Do not misunderstand. There is dignity in human labor. It can be positively creative. It often contributes to the well-being of society. It certainly provides the essentials of survival for our families.

But we often lose perspective on the legitimate meaning of work. We become obsessed by how much we can earn as a sign of what we can buy, as a seal of our self-importance.

None of us are exempt from such temptations. *All* of us are bombarded by TV and magazine ads which tempt us to see material goods as symbols of our status. (Have you seen the one where the woman eats all the ice cream with some unpronounceable foreign name, and then we are told to "enjoy the guilt"?) *All* of us are assaulted by signs of status which have nothing to do with usefulness. Just step back from the rear-end labels on designer jeans, for a minute, and ask what possible utility that quarter-inch piece of cloth has for a simple pair of pants!

If we allow ourselves to get caught up in seeing wealth as a sign of worth, we may overextend our working efforts to the detriment of playtime! Or, our play will become just another status symbol, in which the gadgets get in the way of play. In reality, simple gifts of friends, family, and creation have no heavy price tag. They are priceless!

We are all children of God. We need no other status. As Ecclesiastes said, "Better one hand full and peace of mind, than both fists full and toil that is chasing the wind."

3. *The third mistake we make is to think our works will win salvation.* One of the chief battles of the Reformation was fought over this issue. Both Martin Luther and John Calvin protested against a legalistic, mechanical mentality about human behavior which thought, in effect, if I throw some poor peasant a coin, God "owes me one." Fifteenth-century piety had degenerated into a kind of celestial batting average: If you achieve so many hits and so many runs, you can cancel out some of your errors! God had become the Peter Ueberroth of the ecclesiastical set!

Such assumptions never disappear from the human psyche. I suspect they still operate in each of us; the *motivation behind* many of our good deeds remains the same. We are trying to prove to ourselves, others, and God that we are "good people." And we overextend ourselves in the process.

Each of us can think of examples: I receive a call from the PTA asking me to bake something for the election day bakesale. I say yes, even though I know I already have a busy week at the office, my son has a cold and needs pampering, and my folks are visiting for the weekend. So what am I trying to prove? And to whom? The Good News of Jesus Christ, seen clearly by the apostle Paul, recaptured by Luther and Calvin, is that we are accepted by God through our faith and trust in God's gracious love. That's it. We do not have to prove ourselves. We *cannot* prove ourselves, because we will fail. We are loved anyway.

This Good News is not a license for self-indulgence or a dispensation from duty. As God has loved us, we are called to love each other—to become mirrors of God's love. But the *motivation* changes. No longer do we make fifty sandwiches for the urban soup kitchen because we are proving how good we are. We do it as a gift, freely and graciously given. We choose to give of ourselves in freedom, not bondage. And we also are free to say no occasionally, to give ourselves enough spare time for rest, recreation, relations, and reflection.

Here, then, are three tendencies which cause us to lead lives of imbalance: we place performance before people; we see wealth as a sign of worth; we think our "good works" will win our salvation.

If these are the problems, then what does a life rightly lived look like? The clue is *balance* between life as gift and task. It is possible to err on either side. Indeed, some of us are better at playing than at working. But in this hurried, competitive, pressurized era, I suspect that more of us neglect the playfulness which celebrates God's gifts in life. The theme song of our age is "Sister Can You Spare the Time?"

Episcopal Bishop John Coburn has said that the failure to play periodically is a serious sin. I concur.

God is known not only in the serious and the sorrowful but also in the joyous and the playful times in our lives. If we want to be open fully to God's love and leading, we need to spare the time. As we do so, we may become more fully, faithfully human. In turn, we can reflect God's love to others and see God's love in others.

The next time someone asks, "Can you spare the time?" think before you answer. It could change your life.

PRAYER

Dear God, Who makes us lie down in green pastures and Who leads us beside still waters, restore my soul. Help me to spare the time for this good and proper use. Fill me with Your love when I do. Let me play, as well as pray, in Jesus' name.
Amen.

⋙ 5 ⋘

Word Wars

The value of *conflict* as an inevitable and necessary ingredient in authentic Christian living; its place in friendship as the foundation of true unity; problems of and guidelines for *discernment;* the *presence of God* in the midst of conflict as *comforter, judge, reconciler.*

---

2 Corinthians 7:5-13; 5:16-21

Christians in conflict: I suspect many of us think these are mutually exclusive ways of being. Yet we periodically find ourselves ("good church people" that we are) in verbal conflict situations, "word wars," with all the accompanying verbal flair of a Luke Skywalker. We enter these verbal battles with our bosses, with our spouses, with our kids, with our neighbors, with our friends; in our homes, in our workplaces, and, yes, even in our churches.

That we experience verbal conflict, that we sometimes start it, the honest among us dare not deny. Certainly, no discussion of human friendship can be complete without a candid look at one of its almost inevitable ingredients—namely, verbal conflict.

Whether or not the presence of conflict is an automatic indicator of a failure to be faithful Christians, however, is an open question.

Individuals are in conflict. Institutions are in conflict. That conflict is here is clear. Do we like it? Rarely, although sometimes, in retrospect, we say it "clears the air." Do we feel guilty about it? Often, although that does not seem to stop us from "feudin', fussin', and fightin'." *Should* we feel guilty about it? Here's where the answer, from a Christian perspective, gets interesting: sometimes yes, sometimes no, but *always* God is potentially present in the mix—to challenge, to comfort, to chastise, to heal, to forgive.

How, then, should we interpret the value (both negative and positive) of our "word wars"? How can we discern God's will for us in the midst of our conflicts? Let us begin our search for answers to these questions by getting back to a Christian basic—the Scriptures.

When most of us think about Jesus' ministry as recorded in the Four Gospels, we do so through a kind of sentimental, rosy glow. Paintings of Jesus, like the one my grandmother had hanging in her home, show a serene, loving, ethereal countenance—certainly not a man capable of anger, hardly even a man.

I invite you, in your devotional reading, to go back to the Gospels again. This time, underline every example of conflict you encounter. You may be surprised by what you find.

I went on such an exploratory journey recently. Let me share with you a sampling of the types of conflict I discovered.

1. *Conflict between friends.* Remember, for example, the heated exchange between Jesus and Peter about the tragic destiny of the Son of man, in which Jesus rebuked Peter with the words, "Away with you, Satan, . . . you think as men [and women] think, not as God thinks" (Mark 8:33). That was a vigorous exchange! And yet it didn't destroy Jesus' confidence in Peter. In fact, Peter went on to be a cornerstone of the Christian church.

2. *Conflict among the disciples.* On the way to Capernaum, the disciples apparently got into a heated discussion about "who was the greatest." When they arrived at their destination, Jesus asked, "What were you arguing about on the way?" (Mark 9:33-34).

3. *Conflict within the family.* Mark tells us that early in Jesus' ministry, he was harried by crowds and hardly had

time to eat; and we read that "when his family heard of this, they set out to take charge of him; for people were saying that he was out of his mind" (Mark 3:21). Can't you imagine the discussion which went on among Jesus' relatives, before they set out to "rescue him" from his alleged lunacy!

4. *Conflict within a community.* When Jesus healed the Gerasene demoniac, the unfortunate price of restoring this poor insane man to health was to drive the demons out of the man and into "a large herd of pigs feeding on the hill-side" (Mark 5:11). This spectacle was so disturbing to the townspeople that "they begged Jesus to leave the district" (Mark 5:16-17). In other words, they urged him out of town.

5. *Conflicts between religious factions.* The Gospels are peppered with heated discussions between Jesus and the Pharisees, who were determined to catch him in a snare and prove he was a heretic. Bitter words were exchanged, with Jesus calling them "hypocrites," "blind guides," and other equally uncharitable names. One of the best examples we have of this running conflict is Jesus' display of righteous anger when he "went into the temple and drove out all who were buying and selling in the temple precincts . . ." (Matthew 21:12). We can speculate that Jesus was fed up. He had had enough. So he translated his words into actions to make his message visible.

If we move from the Gospels into the Pauline letters (especially First and Second Corinthians and Galatians), we discover that the early church had its share of controversy. Paul is so distressed by the contentious Corinthians that he hardly takes time for a formal greeting. "I have been told," he says, "by Chloe's people that there are quarrels among you" (1 Corinthians 1:11).

And if we move from the Scriptures into the early church, the controversies continue. The ecumenical councils were convened to settle theological disputes. As a matter of fact, it is reported that during the great Christological controversies, "hymns were sung in popular style like rival football 'chants' of today."[1]

This, I suppose, would be the equivalent of the Methodists holding a rally on one side of Madison Square Garden and singing "Onward, Christian Soldiers" at fever pitch, while the Lutherans, with equal vigor, bellowed "A Mighty Fortress Is Our God" from the other end of the building.

The conclusion we are forced to draw from all this data is that in our contemporary conflicts, we may not necessarily be in *good* company, but we sure have plenty of it!

So what are we to make of all this Christian contentiousness? If, as I am convinced, every realm of human experience is a fit subject for theological reflection, then perhaps we can discover fresh meanings about conflict by trying to step back and look at it through the God we know in Jesus Christ.

When we do this, what do we see? We see Jesus—whom we confess to be the Christ, our Lord and Savior, a messenger of divine love—embroiled in conflicts. Paul recognizes this gift in his letter to the Corinthian church, when he asserts that "Christ was innocent of sin, and yet for our sake God made him one with the sinfulness of men [and women], so that in him we might be made one with the goodness of God" (2 Corinthians 5:21).

What an incredibly freeing gift this is! Jesus walked to the outer limits, the very extremities of human existence, to show us that no experience of ours is beyond the grasp, the identification, the compassion of God—including experiencing conflict. We are called, then, to accept conflict as a God-given part of human nature, which, like all other gifts, may be used or abused. But we should not always fear its presence. God may be working God's purposes out even in conflict situations.

Conflict and the anger which usually accompanies it are part of what it means to be human. Conflict, in and of itself,

---

[1]Gordon S. Wakefield, ed., *The Westminster Dictionary of Christian Spirituality* (Philadelphia: The Westminster Press, 1983), p. 203.

is not necessarily evil (although sin may lurk in one or more of the participants). In fact, sometimes conflict becomes necessary to assert the good. We may not like conflict. It may get us all churned up inside, but it is not necessarily antithetical to authentic Christian living. Rather, it is part of being human. It is part of interpersonal interactions, even— no, especially—among friends and intimates. It is part of communal life, including the life of the church. Conflict usually is unpleasant, but, like going to the dentist, it may be necessary for the health and integrity of the body.

Though sustained conflict in interpersonal relationships may be a danger sign that outside help and mediation are needed, periodic conflicts are part of the stuff of life and may anchor our souls to each other more firmly.

The eighteenth-century Quaker John Woolman saw this clearly. Woolman was convinced, before the notion became commonplace, that slavery was a great evil which corroded all whom it touched. He felt compelled to witness to this conviction wherever he went. Frequently, it brought him into conflict with his friends. Often, he would be a guest in the home of friends where slaves were kept, and he struggled mightily over whether, and how, to witness to his God-inspired conviction even as he accepted the hospitality of his friends. He spoke of it in his journal, saying, "To see the failings of our friends and think hard on them, without opening that which we ought to open, and still carry a face of friendship—this tends to undermine the foundation of true unity."[2]

Woolman's observation also applies to our churches. I have seen people leave a church at the sign of conflict, disillusioned, hurt, angry because, as they say, "That's not what church is all about. Christians aren't supposed to quarrel."

Clearly, Christians *do* quarrel. One of the lessons of the incarnation seems to be that to fail to accept conflict as an

[2]Douglas V. Steere, ed., *Quaker Spirituality: Selected Writings* (New York: Paulist Press, 1984), p. 198.

45

admittedly unpleasant part of life is to deny our humanity. So, as Christians in community, we are called to accept the virtual inevitability of periodic conflicts, to face them and to *see them through*—all in community. It is the "seeing through" that is the mark of love.

The more difficult question is one of discernment. How can we determine the will of God in the midst of our conflicts? This, after all, is the question we should be asking if we are striving to be faithful. And that leads to a few suggestions.

1. *The ultimate value of conflict, from a Christian perspective, should be to promote reconciliation.* In the words of Paul, "We come therefore as Christ's ambassadors" (2 Corinthians 5:20). And what has Christ done? He "has enlisted us in this service of reconciliation" (v. 18). This is one key way to discern the will of God in conflict situations. And if the *ultimate* aim of reconciliation is lacking, it is also a way of recognizing genuine, intractable evil.

If you find yourself warming up to an argument with a friend almost for the sheer fun of it—because you had a bad day at the office, or you were feeling bored and "out of sorts"—in all probability, the chief aim of the battle is release, not reconciliation. If God is present in this situation, it is probably to tell you that you need a vacation! But if you are honest with yourself, you can test your motives (or those of your friend) against the standard of God's call to be an ambassador of reconciliation and judge the value of the conflict accordingly.

On the other hand, think back to the Quaker John Woolman for a minute. He was caught in a dilemma between his love for his friends and his loyalty to God. Woolman was convinced, in the core of his being, that slavery was an abomination in the sight of the Lord. So Woolman *had no choice* but to risk short-term conflict with his slave-owning friends in order to promote long-term reconciliation for *all* of humanity—black and white alike. The ultimate value of Woolman's conflict was the promotion of reconciliation. To have glossed over such a grievous source of pain would have made a sham of friendship. So Woolman took the risk.

The same dynamic may occur in church circles. Look, for example, at the ecumenical movement, an effort to reconcile our divided churches. If, in our eager longing to make visible our oneness in Christ Jesus, we pretend that our disagreements do not exist (whether over the issue of abortion, or the nature of ministry, or the proper structure of church life), we are, to use Woolman's words, "undermining the foundation of true unity." Or if we "hold hands" during the Week of Prayer for Christian Unity but throw verbal spitballs at each other from a safe distance during the rest of the year, we will not move our churches toward reconciliation.

Papering over real disagreements or indulging in them at a safe distance is easy and unproductive. The cost of discipleship in interchurch relationships may mean short-term conflict to promote long-term reconciliation.

Reconciliation is the key concept. The Gospels are saturated with a plea for love restored to its rightful place in human relations. But the plea for reconciliation presupposes that we have divisions. We cannot escape the hard work, often the conflict, necessary to achieve the aim of reconciliation.

2. *The means of verbal conflict, from a Christian perspective, should be modest and fair.* If, as we confess every Sunday morning at the beginning of worship, all of us are frail, fallible, and fallen, then none of us consistently has a corner on the truth. Thus, if we are interested in *finding* the truth, we should strive to be open to new insights, fresh discoveries, different perspectives. We cannot do this if we cling rigidly to our convictions, regardless of the evidence, like children who are unable to move beyond flinging, " 'Tis not!" " 'Tis so!" at each other repeatedly, with jaws out and tongues flailing. Modesty—i.e., having a realistic assessment of one's abilities and limitations—is the best policy.

Modesty must be coupled with fairness. If the purpose of conflict is to discern the will of God, we will discipline ourselves not to be concerned about who "wins" and who "loses." Rather, our quest will be a search for the truth or else the best possible solution in a situation where the truth is elusive and ambiguous. Or, if nothing seems clear, we will keep open the lines of communication until a resolution is possible.

All these aims, however, presuppose fairness, which translates into certain "commandments of communication in conflict," such as the following: Thou shalt not misrepresent the position of thine opponent. Thou shalt not bring extraneous issues into an argument. Thou shalt not engage in character assassination. Thou shalt not withhold relevant data from the debate. I am sure you can think of other rules to add to this list.

The devil must dance with glee over our battling behavior, because our sinful natures so often get the better of us. If, when your spouse complains that you are not carrying your share of domestic chores, you retort that he or she is too fat anyway and needs the extra exercise, you have brought an extraneous issue into the argument. You are not fighting fairly. You are interested in winning, not discerning the truth.

The means of verbal conflict should be modest and fair if our aim is to discern the will of God.

3. *The conclusion of verbal conflict, from a Christian perspective, should include forgiveness,* "seventy times seven" (Matthew 18:22), if necessary. God has no illusions about us, and yet God's grace is open to all who come with repentant hearts. This, then, becomes a model for *human* behavior—in the family, among friends, in the church, among the nations. The issue of forgiveness was so important that Jesus gave it a prominent place in prayer—"forgive us our debts, *as we forgive our debtors.*" And it became one of his last earthly acts: "Father, forgive them; they do not know what they are doing" (Luke 23:34).

We are called to imitate this divine behavior, as a sign of God's love and a means of reconciliation which is at the heart of the gospel. God is present whenever genuine forgiveness is manifested. Forgiveness is a sign of faithfulness.

These, then, are three guidelines to help us determine the will of God in the midst of our conflicts.

So the next time you find yourself putting on your "Luke Skywalker" hat for a session of "Word Wars," remember: there's ample precedent in the incarnation. Then stop and ask yourself: what is God saying in the midst of this? And try to listen to God's leadings. You may be surprised by where they take you.

PRAYER

Dear God, loving Lord, Who has befriended us in our brokenness and our fragility through the gift of Your Son, our Friend, Jesus Christ, help me to be open to Your Spirit in times of conflict. Enable me to examine these trials unafraid and to be receptive to Your presence, Your power, Your proddings even then. Help me to seek Your will, not my own. Grant me wisdom, grant me courage, whenever I find myself in conflict. This I humbly ask in the name of Christ. Amen.

⟶≫ 6 ≪⟵
Love and Death

The challenge of *loss* as a tragic element in human existence; the danger of *despair,* the role of *duty,* the embracing of *hope;* the power of friendship despite death, and the importance of living friendships in the midst of death; the presence and power of a *God who suffers with us,* as shown by the cross.

Genesis 24:62-67; Romans 8:26-39

We do not ordinarily think of the contemporary playwright/humorist Woody Allen and the biblical patriarch Isaac as having anything in common. But it has occurred to me that, despite the centuries between them, both saw the relationship between love and death.

Allen produced a film on the subject. In it, he cavorts with the leading lady and stumbles haphazardly—as only Woody Allen can—into various life-threatening situations. The movie is a metaphor of love and loss.

And in the Book of Genesis, we read the story of Isaac's arranged marriage to Rebekah, who was the ancient Near-Eastern equivalent to a "mail-order bride." The Bible tells us, "So she [Rebekah] became his [Isaac's] wife, and he loved her and was consoled for the death of his mother" (v. 67).

Love and death. The relationship imposed itself on my mind recently when I had a conversation with a man who was wrestling with the pain which comes from loving and losing. He was grieving over the death of his father—a death that left loneliness, guilt, and anger behind. Some of the

unresolved pain had spilled over into his living relationships, with threatening consequences. He was in danger of
despair.

It seems that we human beings, relational creatures that
we are, find ourselves caught in a dilemma. Love—among
parents and children, spouses, or friends—gives life its deepest meaning. Yet love entails risk, because sooner or later, in
one way or another, relationships stumble into the curtain
of mortality.

Since we have no choice but to accept this curious juxta-
position, how can Christians understand it in ways that
enhance, rather than inhibit, life? And where, on earth, is
the God we know in Christ as we career from love to death
and back again?

In Bishop John Coburn's book *A Life to Live—A Way to Pray,*
he ends one chapter with the question, "If you knew that the
hour of your death was tomorrow, how would you spend
the next twenty-four hours?"[1] It is no accident that this
question concludes a chapter called "Sexuality, Death, and
Love." Bishop Coburn expects that, for most of us, the answer to his question would be *relational.* It would involve
people—friends and/or family who have given life its deepest meaning.

Rollo May has observed that "one of the most profound
and meaningful paradoxes of love . . . is the intensified
openness to love which the awareness of death gives us and,
simultaneously, the increased sense of death which love
brings with it."[2]

Love brings with it an increased sense of death. We do not
want to lose that which is most precious to us, and loving
relationships are the most treasured part of life.

A friend of mine, who also is a single parent, used to call
me, terrified, whenever she put her son on a plane to visit
his father. She was afraid the plane would crash, and she

[1]John B. Coburn, *A Life to Live—A Way to Pray* (New York: The Seabury Press,
1973), pp. 70-71.
[2]Rollo May, *Love and Will* (New York: W.W. Norton & Co., Inc., 1969), p. 99.

would be bereft. She knew she would get a sympathetic hearing, because I have experienced similar feelings. We used to joke about the feelings being different when we traveled with our children. Then, we would think, if an accident occurred, both mother and child would be dead, and neither would be left behind to mourn the loss! It was a crazy kind of comfort! Love brings with it an increased sense of death.

The awareness of death potentially intensifies our openness to love. When we do not feel that we have "all the time in the world," how we use the time we *do* have takes on new meaning. This awareness, we are told, is a primary factor underlying some of the upheaval which seems to accompany birthdays in "mid-life."

When I turned forty, I received the usual collection of cards making light of this undeniable entrance into middle age. I also was given a poem, which illustrates with humor and insight how death changes our perspective on life. The poem follows, complete with spicy language:

The Second Half

> I turned forty
> awhile ago
> and came dribbling out
> of the locker room
> ready to start
> the second half
> glancing up
> at the scoreboard
> i saw that we
> were behind
> 7 to 84
> and it came to me then
> we ain't gonna win
> and
> considering the score

i'm beginning
to be damn glad
that this particular
game
ain't gonna go on
forever

but don't take this
to mean
i'm ready
for the showers

take it to mean
i'm probably
gonna play
one hellava
second half

i told this
to some kids
in the court next to mine
and they laughed
but i don't think
they understood
how could they
playing
in the
first quarter
only one point
behind[3]

Poet Ric Masten says he's "glad that this particular game ain't gonna go on forever." But he's determined to "play one hellava second half." And the Christian faith tells us that our relationships with the other players on the team make a major difference in the quality of our game. Abraham Maslow said, "I wonder if we could love passionately, if

[3]Ric Masten, *Speaking Poems* (Boston: Beacon Press, 1977), p. 49. Used by permission.

ecstasy would be possible at all, if we knew we'd never die."[4] The awareness of death potentially intensifies our openness to love.

Loving human relationships also can be the cushion which softens the blow of death. Those who have experienced the grief of loss know what potentially soothing, comforting, healing power is in a warm hug, a caring smile, a listening ear, a spontaneous visit. Those who've baked casseroles, pies, and cookies for a bereaved friend or relative and those who have been the recipients of such substance know how much nurture can be experienced through that simple sign of friendly care.

Recently I was leafing through the journal of a Quaker leader, Rufus Jones, who wrote the following in his diary not long after he lost his son:

> When my sorrow was at its most acute stage I was walking along a great city highway [Birmingham], when suddenly I saw a little child come out of a great gate, which swung to and fastened behind her. She wanted to go to her home behind the gate, but it would not open. She pounded in vain with her little fist. She rattled the gate. Then she wailed as though her heart would break. The cry brought the mother. She caught the child in her arms and kissed away the tears. "Didn't you know I would come? It is all right now." All of a sudden I saw with my spirit that there was love behind my shut gate.
>
> Yes, "where there is so much love, there must be more."[5]

Jones came to understand the love of God by being hospitable to the potential for love within himself and those around him. Such is the legacy of love, even in the midst of the tragedy of death. Loving human relationships are the cushion which softens the blow of death.

And undergirding all these is the compassionate, forgiving, healing love of God, working in us, through us, around

---

[4]Quoted in May, *Love and Will,* p. 99.
[5]Steere, *Quaker Spirituality,* p. 274.

us—a love, as we proclaim in one of the hymns we sing, that "will not let [us] go."

The apostle Paul testifies to the power of this love in his letter to the Roman church. In it Paul poses a relentless series of questions: "If God is on our side, who is against us? He did not spare his own Son, but surrendered him for us all; and with this gift how can he fail to lavish upon us all he has to give?" (8:31–32). "Then what can separate us from the love of Christ?" (v. 35).

Then Paul gives his answer. In one of the most moving testimonies in all of Scripture, Paul says: "For I am convinced that there is nothing in death or life, in the realm of spirits or superhuman powers, in the world as it is or the world as it shall be, in the forces of the universe, in heights or depths—nothing in all creation that can separate us from the love of God in Christ Jesus our Lord" (vv. 38–39).

Therein lies our ultimate comfort. "We can fall no deeper than God's arms can reach, however deep we fall."[6] The God who is with us is with us always—especially in our sufferings. Even in the midst of death—most assuredly in the midst of death—God's love will triumph. Such is the power of God.

The awareness of our mortality poses a challenge to each of us. It calls us to maximize the use of the love we keep "behind our shut gates." The very love which entails the risk of loss also has the power to give life its deepest meanings, here and now, in whatever state we find ourselves.

And for those who mourn on this side of the grave, they are blessed when they are comforted by God's love made tangible through human beings like you and me. Such is the relationship between love and death.

PRAYER ⋘

Dear God, You who love us with a love that will not let us go, bring my anxieties about the fragility of life into Your

[6]*Ibid.*, p. 237.

Holy Presence. Be with me in my confusion and my fear. Enable me to be hospitable to the love within myself and others as a sign of Your own compassionate, healing love, which gives life now and forever. In the name of Jesus Christ, our Redeemer, I pray.
Amen.

⟶≫ 7 ≪⟵

Greatheart

The importance of cultivating *spiritual companionship* to facilitate faith journeys—its common neglect in the scope of human friendship, its value in *strengthening our personal pilgrimage of faith,* its obligation as part of our *vocation given in Christian baptism.*

Proverbs 20:5; Hebrews 12:1-2

I do not know how many contemporary Christians are familiar with John Bunyan's *Pilgrim's Progress.* I probably would not be if I had not been encouraged to read it in seminary. But this seventeenth-century Puritan classic about the life-long Christian spiritual journey is filled with characters—No-Heart, Short-Wind, Linger-After-Lust, Sleepy-Head, Dull—whose personalities and problems have a timeless ring.

One of the most notable characters in *Pilgrim's Progress* is Greatheart. Bunyan chooses Greatheart, a servant in the household of Interpreter, to "take sword, and helmet, and shield," and to serve as a companion to the Christian pilgrims on their long, arduous, sometimes frightening journey to salvation, which happened—and happens for us, as well —to be a life-long trip.

What does Greatheart do? He converses. He shares from the rich storehouse of his own Christian experience. He walks beside. Through his counsel, he sometimes protects. He patiently stays, through thick and thin, to the very end of the journey, when the pilgrims are about to cross the river into the bosom of God. In short, Greatheart was a Christian friend.

Friendship in Christ—what might this mean? Who is called to such a vocation? What does it involve?

To be a Christian friend means that we consciously share our personal quest to know and to radiate the love of God with the one whom we are befriending. If you think this smacks of witness and evangelism, you are right. But I do not mean the Bible-thumping, club 'em over the head, "my belief's better than yours" variety. Instead, I'm talking about companionship which does not shrink from including experiences of our quest for God and truth in the conversation.

I am struck by how *infrequently* this occurs among us today. I have felt the lack, on occasion, in my own relationships. All too often, we feel embarrassed and shy about revealing ourselves in what are, admittedly, very intimate ways. And yet, if we do not, we close off one possible avenue for growth in our own faith, and we deny the possibility of enriching the religious life of another.

Let me give you an example of what I mean by such conscious sharing. It comes from my own congregation. A few years ago, during some congregational hearings preceding our minister's call, something happened in the life of the congregation which went beyond the immediate issue at hand. In the course of those meetings, a number of people talked about their own faith experiences in some very remarkable ways. People who, for me, previously had been two-dimensional—limited to the "Hi, how are you" coffee-hour conversations—became depth sources of admiration and inspiration for my own spiritual pilgrimage. They shared from their "great hearts," and in so doing, the whole community was nurtured and enriched. These events provided a glimpse of what it means to be a Christian friend. Let me repeat: To be a *Christian* friend means that we *consciously share* our personal quest to know and to radiate the love of God with the one, or ones, whom we befriend.

All of us—whether lay or ordained—are called, through Christian baptism, to this vocation. Ministers do not have a corner on the market.

I sometimes get the sense that we have mentally created separate rooms in the household of God—one for "amateurs," another for "professionals"—with the attendant assumption that the pros are better at the telling about and the practicing of faith than the amateurs.

It is not so—or it should not be! Baptism claims us for Christ—*all* of us. Through baptism, we are called to Christ in a never-ending quest in which we, like the pilgrims in John Bunyan's book, *may* make progress, but we also stumble and fall, take wrong turns and detours, get tired and distracted, silly and self-centered, along the way—*all* of us, lay and ordained. In view of our stumbling steps, the journey might seem a little less frustrating and frightening if each of us reached out and grabbed someone else's hand, just as "Greatheart" did.

Think, for a minute, about how we use those terms, "amateur" and "professional," when it comes to sports. The Boston Celtics are "pros"—they're "Number One" (at least, most years!), and they get paid for what they do. But do they love the sport any more than a so-called "amateur" basketball team in the Olympics or an "amateur" team at the local high school? I doubt it. Career choices separate the two groups—not necessarily differences in love of the sport.

So it is with Christians. Career choices may separate clergy and lay people, but these do not necessarily dictate differences in our love of God and our call to live a life of love. All of us—whether lay or ordained—are called, through Christian baptism, to be Christian friends.

Christian friendship also involves companionship, not superiority. No one "has all the answers."

A full Christian life includes private prayer, public worship, and servanthood in family and society. In all these realms, however, we are involved in "reaching toward" rather than "arriving at." In prayer, we may experience some times when we have nothing to give God but our poor, tired, broken selves. At other times, we can offer our joy and thanksgiving. And still others, our doubts, fears, and needs.

In worship, sometimes we go because we want to, sometimes because we have to, sometimes out of habit. On occasion, the liturgy may stir us to a profound sense of penitence and praise. Then again, we may feel bored and unmoved.

In servanthood, at times, we may feel like models of faithfulness at home, at work, at play. Or again, we may feel out-of-sync, or inadequate in the face of the trials and tragedies of life, or just plain guilty because we have done things which we know we ought not to have done.

All of this is the stuff of faith. *All* this comes within the sphere of the merciful love of God. None of us are experts in the quest. All of us have experiences which, if shared, may help someone else in his or her journey of faith.

The *only* difference among Christians in our spiritual journeys is the varying degrees to which we are consciously involved in "exercising our spiritual muscles." The writer of Hebrews spoke of running "with perseverance the race that is set before us . . ." (Hebrews 12:1, RSV). Just as you train for months (probably years) if you plan to run in a marathon, so it is with a life of Christian devotion. We cannot learn about the full potential and meaning of prayer if we do not pray or if we pray only occasionally. We will not appreciate the full power of a Christian community if we go to church only at Easter and Christmas.

The more open we are to the Holy Spirit, the more we have to share with others. But just as the most practiced runners sometimes ache, or stumble and fall, or resist the discipline, so it is with the Christian athlete. Thus, Christian friendship involves companionship, not superiority. No one has all the answers. We are, at best, partners in pilgrimage.

These, then, are three facets of Christian friendship: conscious sharing of our personal religious quests; recognition that *all* are called to this vocation; and acknowledgment that Christian friendship involves companionship, not superiority.

I am not saying that you should go out and accost the mail carrier to tell him or her about your faith experiences. Such sharings are, indeed, intimate and come with a level of comfort in a relationship that develops usually over time. I *am* saying that if and when we have such friends, we should not exclude our own faith pilgrimages from the relationship. The book of Proverbs includes this wise saying:

> Counsel in another's heart is like deep water,
> but a discerning man [or woman] will draw it up.
> —Proverbs 20:5

Christian friends are called to imitate Greatheart, who walked beside, sharing from the treasury of his own Christian experience. This is what it means to be a companion on the life-long journey to salvation.

PRAYER
Dear God, You have blessed us with the gift of baptism as a sign and seal of our common calling in Christ. Grant me the grace to embrace this calling as a Christian companion. Help me to share freely and learn fully, drinking from the deep waters of human experiences in the journey of faith. In the name of Jesus Christ I pray.
Amen.

Section 3

From Friends to Neighbors: A Look at Responsible Christian Lifestyles

⇢⟫⟫ 8 ⟨⟨⟵

Slinking Toward Jerusalem

The *quest for congruence* between beliefs and living patterns—Jesus Christ as a model of selflessness; the challenge of Christ to live responsibly; the implications of this challenge in any context.

Isaiah 53; Luke 6:38-49; 11:42

Traditionally, Lent is a forty-day season of spiritual struggle. It is a time when we ponder our flaws and failings, our hopes and accomplishments, our loves and losses, and seek transformation in conformity with the will of God, through self-discipline aided by God's grace. This process, at its best, goes on both in the life of each one of us and in our lives as a community of the faithful. Thus, many take on special devotional exercises of fasting, prayer, and service during this season. For the same reason, people sometimes gather together for fellowship, study, and prayer.

In some worship services, the weekly Lenten Scripture readings have a pattern which reviews the life of Jesus as a model for our own lives. So how do we measure up? How many of us would be comfortable seeing *our* lifestyle elevated as a model of Christian behavior, to be emulated by others?

I do not know about you, but I must confess that when I shut my eyes and put myself right next to Jesus at the beginning of the Jerusalem road in that spring marathon leading to the cross, he sprints, while I slink. My "runner's cramps"—the cause of this unusual gait—are prompted by an honest look at my own "lifestyle."

I used to make fun of my mother's guilt-inducing injunction to "remember the starving children in India" when I stubbornly refused to eat one of her gooey casseroles. She won. I ate the casseroles. I've got the hips to prove it. And that did not help the starving children of India.

Her remedy may have been wrong, but perhaps her concern for a responsible lifestyle wasn't so far off the mark, after all. I think about it now, when I occasionally toss out a moldy leftover from some forgotten corner of my refrigerator. As I scrape the stuff into the garbage, flashes of televised African famine victims run through my mind.

I am not the only one to ponder the issue of responsible lifestyles. *Boston Globe* columnist Ellen Goodman recently wrote about her regular practice of abandoning all use of credit cards during January, and, in her words, giving "up buying anything that I might loosely and subjectively describe as 'unnecessary.' " She describes it as a "phony moral vow: Let's all pretend that we are beyond the reach of crass material values and abandon consumerism for a month just for the virtue of it." And what does she accomplish? "For a brief 31 days," she says, "I rediscover that there is nothing like cash to focus the mind . . . ," as I contemplate "the meaning of the word 'necessary.' "[1]

Join me, then, on the beginning of a journey down the Jerusalem road, during which we can ponder *our* lifestyles. I must warn you, though, that on this journey, I am a fellow-traveler, not a guide. I am confident that the quality of our lifestyles raises important questions. Christ poses them for us. I'm far less sanguine about having figured out the answers.

Considerable confusion exists about the meaning of the term "lifestyle." In sociology, it applies to group patterns of daily life in areas such as family, work, schooling, and community associations. From the standpoint of Christian ethics, we combine *observation* with *valuation,* raising questions about the degree to which our daily living patterns correspond to the Christian values we profess.

In addition to issues of personal behavior, "lifestyles" also have corporate implications. Churches, also, have "lifestyles." How do the ways we live, as *churches—communities* of the faithful—correspond to our proclaimed commitments? For example, how do we as churches spend our money? What do our programs say about what is important to us?

Further, in what ways do we implement our private commitments as public policies (for example, by enacting a Bottle Bill, or a Clean Air Act, to translate private environmental concerns into policies only realizable through public consensus, commitment, and enforcement). What is our *national* lifestyle?

One other point will complete this definitional discourse: Value judgments about lifestyles presuppose that we are *free* to make choices about how to live. Those who live in desperate poverty or in rigidly totalitarian governments have very restricted options. You can only talk about changing lifestyles when you have freedom and options.

[1]Ellen Goodman, "Cutting Off the Card," in *The Boston Globe,* January 29, 1985, p. 13.

Every time I reread the Four Gospels, I am struck anew by Jesus' single-minded devotion to the will of God in all that he said and did. Jesus claimed Isaiah's suffering-servant image as his own and wore it like a mantle, boldly, bravely striding toward Jerusalem. This is the model Jesus sets before us—a model of selflessness. Jesus was a man who lived for others. This was his lifestyle.

Oh, he was human, all right. He sweated and got angry and laughed and agonized, like the rest of us. But he *lived* his words—he was known by his fruit—and that coherence of good heart and good deeds, of loving God and doing justice, was so tight that he rang true in tones the whole world still hears.

His words wash over us, posing questions, challenging us to be authentic and responsible: "You are salt to the world. And if salt becomes tasteless, how is its saltness to be restored?" (Matthew 5:13). "Do not store up for yourselves treasure on earth, where it grows rusty and moth-eaten, and thieves break in to steal it. . . . For where your [treasure] is, there will your heart be also" (Matthew 6:19, 21). "You cannot serve God and Money" (Matthew 6:24). "Therefore I bid you put away anxious thoughts about food and drink to keep you alive, and clothes to cover your body" (Matthew 6:25). "If anyone wishes to be a follower of mine, he [or she] must leave self behind; he [or she] must take up his [or her] cross and come with me" (Matthew 16:24). "A rich man [or woman] will find it hard to enter the kingdom of Heaven" (Matthew 19:23). "Whoever wants to be great must be your servant, and whoever would be first must be the willing slave of all—like the Son of Man . . ." (Matthew 20:26-28).

What can we say about these words? What was Jesus, whom we claim as Christ, telling us about the way we are supposed to live? Theologians and ethicists and biblical scholars have spent centuries and volumes unpacking these words, and I bow in humble respect before their efforts.

Nevertheless, since every Christian is called to embody this message in a very personal, intimate way, let me share some of my own observations.

First, when Jesus urges us not to store up for ourselves treasures on earth, he seems to be speaking to those who have them, more than those who do not. The words are targeted. I doubt that he would allow those who are well fed, well clothed, well housed, well entertained, to point our fingers complacently at the poor and say that the basic necessities of life don't matter. Instead, he seems to be saying such things do matter, but they matter equally for everyone. Those who live adequately should not be so weighted down by their "earthly treasures" that they are not willing to share them, since the treasures are, in some sense, gifts of God to begin with. In other words, if the shoe fits, do not wear it, share it!

Second, I suspect that Jesus meant what he said. Over the years, a lot of ink has been spilled to soothe our consciences and protect our purses. Someone once told me about a prudent Presbyterian pastor who used to preach a yearly sermon to his wealthy congregation on the theme "It isn't *money* that's the root of all evil; it's the *love* of it." Well, in one sense, that's true. But if any of his millionaire congregants went walking away from church thinking, "Well, I don't *love* my money, so I can do as I please with it and go merrily about my business," then the gospel got distorted.

Jesus preached a radical ethic of love and justice and compassion and selflessness—so hard that none of us ever can fully measure up to it. But we cannot let ourselves off the obligatory hook by diluting the ethic. Instead, God keeps us on the hook—God expects great things from us—while at the same time, God recognizes our inadequacies and loves us anyway. That is called grace, and it is held in ongoing tension with a sense of responsibility flowing out of God's love for us.

Third, Jesus seemed to recognize the seductive nature of material goods. When he observed that "a rich man [person] will find it hard to enter the kingdom of Heaven" (Matthew 19:23), I suspect that's what he had in mind. There's something entrapping and spiritually sapping about the "thingness" of our society—a "consumerism" and "materialism" in which *all* of us are caught. Those who are poor see the lifestyles of those who are not and want the trappings—the "Cabbage Patch" doll which was a recent Christmas rage (I heard on the radio not long ago that the latest is orthodontal work, to get your doll's teeth straightened!); the video equipment which no home can "afford" to be without. None of us are fully exempt from these allures; we just keep different "must" lists. The thought of moving and packing up the years of accumulated items in my house may keep me permanently ensconced where I am!

Whether we have these things, or want to have them, our lives often are complicated—and encumbered—by our possessions in ways that, from a Christian perspective, put us "out of focus" as spiritual beings. Thus, it becomes more difficult "to enter the kingdom of Heaven." The way is too cluttered.

And fourth, Jesus did seem to display, in the words of Pope John Paul II, a "preferential option for the poor." Jesus took the assumptions of his society about who was "right with God" and turned them totally around. He said, in effect, wealth and outward appearances of piety are not automatic indicators of one's favor with God. In fact, those whom society often rejects receive *special* favor in God's sight, not because of any inherent moral superiority on their part, but *because of their great need.*

Even more important, however, is the conclusion Jesus draws from this understanding of God. If the poor and the rejected in the world receive special favor in God's sight, the rest of us are supposed to put on God's glasses when we look at the world. And when we do that, all of a sudden, the faceless throngs become individual human beings of dignity and worth, in need of love, deserving compassion, *just like us.* No longer can we walk down the Jerusalem road with our eyes narrowly focused on the cross. The cross itself forces us to expand our vision—to see what is going on in the lives of others along the way. This, I believe, is what Jesus meant when he chastised the Pharisees with the words, "You pay tithes of mint and rue and every garden-herb, but have no care for justice and the love of God" (Luke 11:42).

These, then, are some beginning observations about Jesus' words concerning the way we live: when he urges us not to store up treasures on earth, he speaks "contextually," i.e., to those who have them. He preaches a radical ethic which should not be diluted. He recognizes how difficult it is to measure up—how seductive material goods can be. And he shows special concern for the poor.

So what does all this mean for us, here and now?

Let me offer a few observations:

1. When Christians contemplate changing our lifestyles, *we do so in an effort to seek greater congruence between what we believe and how we live.* At heart, this is a quest for discipleship, which Episcopal Bishop John Coburn says "is a sign that you have made a choice to live in a certain way." Coburn continues, "We experience our greatest power for living when we are willing *not* to get our own way because we love another."[2] Such willingness to free ourselves from certain ways of living is the way of Christ. Thus, we are free to respond to God's law of love.

Gustavo Gutierrez also picks up this theme in his book *We Drink from Our Own Wells.* Gutierrez unpacks the term "the way," a synonym for "discipleship," which appears prominently in both Acts and the Pauline letters. "To follow the way is to practice a certain conduct," Gutierrez says. "What is meant is conduct in the service of God."[3]

2. Both Coburn and Gutierrez see neighbor love writ large on a global canvas. *A Christlike lifestyle not only involves individual*

<hr />

[2]John B. Coburn, *A Life to Live—A Way to Pray* (New York: The Seabury Press, 1973), p. 57.

[3]Gustavo Gutierrez, *We Drink from Our Own Wells* (Maryknoll, N.Y.: Orbis Books, 1984), p. 81.

acts of human kindness and Christian charity; it reaches beyond these to abstract forms of love, where the expressions and the impact often are not tangible or immediate. If, for example, we adjust our lifestyles to consume less energy in our homes and churches, our individual acts combine with millions of others giving *future* generations access to finite supplies of fossil fuels.

3. *Our lifestyles, both individual and corporate, have implications for evangelism.* They are living testimony to our faith commitments. They speak, by example, to a secular world. Take, for example, a corporate illustration: the pattern of life of our churches—divided, sometimes competitive, often duplicative.

I became more aware than ever before of the "public" face of the church in 1983, while studying at the World Council of Churches' Ecumenical Institute outside Geneva. Gathered there were thirty clergy and laity from all over the world, many of whom were first- or second-generation converts to Christianity, inspired and imbued with a love of Christ by missionaries sent from churches like ours. In some cases, the conversions had been quite dramatic. You should have seen my son's face when a gentle Indonesian pastor told him that this pastor's grandfather had been a headhunter! That conversion was life-affirming in a very concrete way! Christ's message got through: chopping off people's heads and loving God are mutually exclusive propositions! You cannot do one and be the other. God is love, and God calls us to reflect this reconciling, healing love in all our relationships. That is the core of Christ's message.

As we talked with African and Asian Christian colleagues, however, it appeared to them that the message of our missionaries was a bit muddled. If the gospel—the Good News —is an appeal to reconciling love, then why is it so terribly important to convert—not just to Christianity—but to Methodist Christianity or to Baptist Christianity or to Episcopal Christianity? We seem, to them, to be putting fences around our love. Does this mirror the love of God?

"Bring us your Divine Word," they say, "but leave your divisions at home. We do not need them." Our denominationalism does not make sense to them, and the competitive rivalries of earlier generations of missionaries—now, mercifully dropped by most—have left institutional dilemmas in their wake.

These new Christians see clearly what many of us only dimly perceive. All too often, there is a basic inconsistency between our message and our ministry. Our corporate lifestyle lacks coherence. We proclaim reconciliation, yet frequently we have been quite comfortable with the divisions among our churches. When these divisions are transplanted to foreign soil, where Christians sometimes are a small minority, the separations make no sense and complicate their task of witness and evangelism. Actions speak louder than words. This is a good example, then, of how our institutional lifestyle affects our mission efforts.

I'm sure you can think of interpersonal examples as well, of people whose lives have been so Christlike that others have been moved—through curiosity, or need, or inspiration —to repentance and conversion. Our lifestyles, then, have implications for evangelism.

So how do we measure up? Are we sprinters or slinkers? The quest for congruence between what we believe and how we live is never-ending. It is the nature of discipleship.

PRAYER

Dear God, Who have revealed Yourself to us in Jesus Christ, a model of selflessness, I come to You with a humble and repentant heart. Many aspects of my lifestyle are not worthy of imitation. Break apart the entrenched patterns to which I cling. Instead, I would cling to You. Open me up to more worthy ways of living. Draw me gently toward the vision of self-giving love shown so clearly in Your Son, our Savior, Jesus Christ.
Amen.

⇢⟫ 9 ⟪⇠

Friends and Neighbors

Some guidelines for achieving congruence—combining
acts of compassion with a quest for justice, coupling an
appreciation for creation with the pursuit of simplicity,
risking engagement in society despite its ambiguities,
struggling to be other-directed, valuing life, and seek-
ing the companionship of friends to strengthen one on
the journey.

Luke 10:25-37; Romans 3:21-26

Our Puritan forebears had one basic guideline of success:
the creation of a Christian community in which their calling to holy living could be fulfilled. Material wealth was—
at least in theory!—not a legitimate criterion. The first gov-
ernor of the Massachusetts Bay Colony, John Winthrop,
finally had to relinquish the post (having served twelve
terms) because he had spent so much time on matters of
the public good that his private estate was near bank-
ruptcy![1]

Winthrop must have been an engaging character.

When it was reported to him during an especially long and
hard winter that a poor man in his neighborhood was stealing from his woodpile, Winthrop called the man into his
presence and told him that because of the severity of the
winter and his need, he had permission to supply himself

---

[1]Robert N. Bellah, Richard Madsen, William M. Sullivan, Ann Swindler, and
Steven M. Tipton, *Habits of the Heart* (Berkeley and Los Angeles: University of
California Press, 1985), p. 29.

from Winthrop's woodpile for the rest of the cold season. Thus, he said to his friends, did he effectively cure the man from stealing.[2]

And thus did Winthrop answer the question "Who is my neighbor?"

This question has a long history, stretching all the way back to the road from Jerusalem to Jericho. After hearing Jesus tell the story of the good Samaritan, the lawyer (who had been pressing for specificity on the issue of neighborliness) answered the question himself. He said the good neighbor was "the one who showed him kindness" (Luke 10:37). And Jesus responded, "Go and do as he did."

In our fallen attempts to circumscribe our obligations to fit our inclinations, we often imitate the legalism of that first-century lawyer. We try to draw a small circle, but Jesus snatches our pen away and circumscribes the whole earth. "Who is my neighbor?" The one or ones who have needs.

And so, we are pushed to examine our living patterns to see how they compare with the good Samaritan. The following are some guidelines to help us begin the process of self-scrutiny.

1. An authentic Christian lifestyle couples individual acts of compassion with a quest for justice. Through contributions to Church World Service, for example, we aid our brothers and sisters who are victims of the famine in Africa. But this tale has another twist as well—one we think of less frequently. According to the Roman Catholic Bishops' Pastoral Letter on the U.S. Economy (first draft),

> From 1981 to 1984 Congressional appropriations for security-related aid programs increased nearly two-thirds, while development assistance appropriations remained almost unchanged . . . the United States, the "inventor" of foreign aid, is now almost at the bottom of the list of industrialized

[2]*Ibid.*

. . . countries in the percentage of gross national product (GNP) devoted to . . . foreign assistance. . . .[3]

This occurs in a country whose per capita income is approximately $12,500, in comparison with "half of the world's population—2 billion people—[who] live in countries where the per capita annual income is $400 or less. . . ."[4]

It is not enough, then, to bind up the wounds of the poor. Our society, which has so much, has a responsibility to help change the conditions which have caused those wounds in the first place. This is an example of what justice requires. And each of us, who are part of this comparative affluence, are called to incorporate these corporate acts of compassion in our self-understanding of what it means to be a responsible Christian.

By advocating such changes in public policy, we hedge our own acquisitiveness. In a sense, we intentionally work against ourselves—by supporting public acts which cost public money that, in the final analysis, comes out of our private pockets. In this way, we enforce acts of corporate compassion which emerge from this self-understanding of what it means to be a responsible Christian. In this way, we combat our corporate sinfulness. An authentic Christian lifestyle couples individual acts of compassion with a quest for justice. Love has obligations.

2. An authentic Christian lifestyle couples a profound, joyous, reverent appreciation for the goodness of God's creation with a quest for simplicity that allows us to savor God's good gifts. We don't need gadgets to revel in the beauty of birds, the satisfactions of parenting, the thrill of ideas exchanged, the sustenance of friends and family, the pleasure of tasty food lovingly prepared (including, I must confess, the raptures of mint chocolate chip ice cream!). In fact, sometimes gadgets get in the way of our ability to appreciate that which really matters. In a curious

[3]National Conference of Catholic Bishops, "First Draft Pastoral Letter on Catholic Social Teaching and the U.S. Economy" (Washington, D.C., November 11, 1984), p. 22, Par. 291.
[4]*Ibid.,* p. 274.

irony, Jesus tells us that we must lose our lives in order to find them. Herein lies the key to contentment—not in things but in a way of *being*.

3. A responsible Christian lifestyle is engaged in society rather than withdrawn from it. We are called to transform culture, not to separate ourselves from it, despite all the risks and ambiguities involved in this process. This understanding is consistent with our Protestant heritage, which challenges everyone to give Christian witness in the context of our everyday domestic and workday world. Even Catholic contemplative Thomas Merton seems to acknowledge the importance of engagement, despite his own withdrawal, in the title of one of his later works, *Conjectures of a Guilty Bystander.* [5]

The great Puritan poet John Milton observed, "I cannot praise a fugitive and cloister'd vertue, unexercis'd and unbreath'd, that never sallies out and sees her adversary, but slinks out of the race, where that immortal garland is to be run for, not without dust and heat."[6]

Indeed, the model Jesus offers is one of engagement, both through his example and his teachings. The parable of the good Samaritan is a story of one who takes risks, who goes out of his way, who reaches beyond custom. Jesus himself did all this and more.

From a theological standpoint, the totality of the Christ event reveals a God who gets involved in the messiness of history, despite the cost and the risk of loss.

Thus, we are on secure ground in "staying in the dust and heat of the race" rather than withdrawing from it.

4. An authentic Christian lifestyle is other-directed, both in space and in time. It examines personal and communal behavior *in light of* the impact that behavior will have on others, across the street, across town, across the state, throughout the nation, around the world, not only now, but also in the future, in

[5]Thomas Merton, *Conjectures of a Guilty Bystander* (Garden City, N.Y.: Doubleday & Co., Inc., 1968).
[6]Gordon S. Wakefield, ed., *The Westminster Dictionary of Christian Spirituality* (Philadelphia: The Westminster Press, 1983), p. 325.

generations who will live, God willing, long after we are dead and buried.

I got a call from a neighbor recently. She began the conversation by asking if I wanted to go to a meeting. (That, I will admit, was her first mistake!) What unfolded was a tale of struggle over the use of an abandoned neighborhood elementary school. Should the school be used to develop low- and moderate-income housing, or shouldn't it? Beyond the thin veneer of her initial arguments against it ("It will disrupt the quality of education"—an argument which puzzled me, since the school building is no longer in use), she finally said, "But our property values will go down!" In reality, this, too, is a spurious argument in our setting, though *even if it had not been,* I believe a strong case could be made for making our neighborhood more economically inclusive. What she really meant, though she did not say it, was, "We don't want *those* people in *our* neighborhood," whoever "those people" turned out to be.

This is a good example of the way in which all of us, periodically, are faced with issues on which we are compelled to take a stand. This is an opportunity for Christian witness to an other-directed lifestyle. Even if we do not seek out opportunities, they come to us, and we must choose.

Sometimes, however, we may not even be aware that we are making choices. I think, for example, of my ignorant purchase of non-biodegradable detergent for years before I realized I was contributing to the pollution of the environment. Or we may be forced to make bad choices because no other option is available. Suppose you live in an area with little or no public transportation. You are forced to use your automobile to travel, even though you're committed to responsible energy use through mass transit.

All of us in the United States are caught up in patterns of living from which we cannot, in the short run, extricate ourselves, even if we want to, and in ways which may harm others in some far corner of the globe, though we may never fully comprehend them. The apostle Paul recognized this, hundred of years ago, when he observed that "all have sinned and fall short of the glory of God . . ." (Romans 3:23, RSV).

Nevertheless, we are called to make "good faith efforts." An authentic Christian lifestyle is other-directed both in space and in time.

5. *A responsible Christian lifestyle values life.* "Then God said, 'Let us make man [and woman] in our own image, after our likeness' " (Genesis 1:26, RSV). "And God saw everything that he [God] had made, and behold, it was very good" (Genesis 1:31, RSV). This understanding of creation as life-affirming carries into the New Testament. "For God so loved the world that he [God] gave his only Son . . ." (John 3:16, RSV). God cares. Life matters.

Thus, how we choose to live our lives matters. How we treat ourselves and others matters. Human beings deserve respect. Our physical bodies deserve respect.

I do not need to catalog the list of ways in which all of us fall short of this vision or struggle toward its attainment. Newspapers, television, magazines, forums, and seminars—all provide a steady barrage of information about ways to change our personal lifestyles. In fact, there is big money in it, including running shops, fitness salons, Smoke-Enders, and slick seminars combating stress. (The price alone makes my blood pressure go up.)

That we should be taking care of our bodies I have no doubt. From a Christian perspective, respect for one's body through healthful living is a means of glorifying God by respecting God's gift of life. It also is a means of serving God by keeping that life in good repair, to the extent that we have this control.

I do, however, have doubts about some secular assumptions about the current quest for fitness, which are incompatible with Christian norms. If physical fitness becomes an end in itself, we run the risk of narcissism. If physical fitness becomes a means to sexual enticement, we are in danger of substituting appearance for substance and of trivializing the nature of human love. If physical fitness becomes a quest for eternal life staving off the grave, we deceive ourselves about the harsh, inevitable reality of death, and we deny ourselves a reasoned confrontation with the promise of Christ for eternal life.

I'm not saying, "Smoke all you want, eat all you want, drink all you want; it doesn't matter." It *does* matter. But be sure it matters for the right reasons. It matters because we are precious in God's sight, and we have promises to keep.

The Christian pilgrimage is a life-long quest, involving choices about how we use the gift of life. Fortunately, we do not make our journeys alone. The spirit of Christ is with us as we meet him in others and in his body, the church. This companionship is important. It finds us when we lose our way; it keeps us from getting too lonely; it corrects us when we are in error; it spurs us from aimless wanderings to intentional actions.

I do not know how many people are familiar with the writings of Philip Jacob Spener. Spener was a seventeenth-century German Pietist. In his most famous work, *Pia Desideria,* [7] he urged his lackluster German parishioners to take more seriously their Christian calling and advocated a Christian lifestyle which avoided cards, dancing, and the theater, as well as moderation in food, drink, and dress.

What struck me most forcefully, however, was Spener's realistic assessment of human nature. Recognizing that we function more faithfully in a context of mutual support, he advocated gathering the more "serious-minded" into "little churches within the church" for Scripture reading and mutual assistance in moral and spiritual growth.

Spener's approach is timeless. Human nature has not changed. Those who are eager to lead responsible Christian lifestyles still benefit from communal support. When it is available, we should use it. Where it is lacking, we can create

[7]Philip Jacob Spener, *Pia Desideria* (Philadelphia: Fortress Press, 1964).

it. Companionship is as important today as it was in Spener's time.

Our lifestyles, then, are private commitments which make public statements more eloquent than any words we might choose. So what are we saying? Of what are we proud that we would want others to imitate? What *one* thing do we want to change, here and now, which, realistically, we can and will change? These are some of the challenges before us as we examine what it means to be both friend and neighbor.

PRAYER ⋘

Gracious God, You who have befriended us in the person of Your Son, Jesus Christ, help me to answer the question "Who is my neighbor?" in ways which are pleasing in Your sight. Release me from my fears, and enable me to expand my horizons, to include all Your good creation in my vision. Give me the longing to be responsible and the will to support this longing. This I ask in the name of Christ. Amen.

Divine Friendship As It Illumines the Human

⟫⟫ 10 ⟪⟪

The Friendly Face of God

A summary exploration of the meaning of friendship as a primary principle for understanding God—the emphasis on *immanence;* the role of the *incarnation* in bridging the gap between God and humanity (evidenced in love, dependability, and forgiveness); the potential for the model of friendship between God and humanity rightly understood, and its import for human relations.

Exodus 33:7-11; John 3:16-17

I have always loved the story of the little girl in Sunday school who was intently focused on a piece of paper, crayon in hand. "What are you drawing?" asked her teacher. "God," was the reply. The teacher gently responded, "But, honey, no one knows what God looks like." "Well, they will when I'm finished," she said as she returned to her task.

This is a simple story with profound implications. It focuses our attention on the mystery of God. Despite all our Sunday morning "God talk," when we are alone at night with a four-year-old child, staring out the window at the starry heavens, and we get asked, "What is God like?" what do we say? Where do we begin?

Our answers are not just a pedagogical exercise. If we are able to dig deep enough into our psyches, beyond the jargon, we will discover a fundamental ordering principle which shapes our attitudes toward life and death, self and neighbor, humanity and cosmos. Our answers to the question "What is God like?" color our lives in profound ways.

The seventeenth-century English Puritan Richard Baxter understood this well. While he was gravely ill, staring death in the face, he shared his vision of God in a book he called *The Saints' Everlasting Rest,* a devotional work treasured by generations of Protestants. Baxter said,

> When our ignorance and unbelief have drawn the most deformed picture of God in our imaginations, then we complain that we cannot love him, nor delight in him. This is the case of many thousand Christians . . . O that we could always think of God as we do of a friend; as of one that unfeignedly loves us, even more than we do ourselves; whose very heart is set upon us to do us good, and hath therefore provided for us an everlasting dwelling with himself!"[1]

"Oh, that we could always think of God as we do of a friend." Baxter hit upon a powerful analogy which Christians through the ages have used again and again: God as our friend. The image of friend has been one primary ordering principle through the centuries for answering the question "What is God like?"

In the Old Testament Scripture cited at the opening of this chapter we hear: "Thus the LORD used to speak to Moses face

[1]Richard Baxter, *The Saints' Everlasting Rest,* abridged by Benjamin Fawcett, A.M. (Boston: Gould, Kindall, and Lincoln, 1845), p. 238.

to face, as a man speaks to his friend" (Exodus 33:11, RSV). Now, they obviously were not "chums," "pals," "good buddies." The encounters between God and Moses always exude an aura of mystery, majesty, and awe. We are talking about the "Holy One of Israel," and the followers of Moses knew it. When Moses went into the tent, we read that "all the people would rise up and worship . . ." (v. 10, RSV).

Yet the God of Moses was not *so* "wholly other" that this divine presence could not be felt in some personal, intimate, understandable ways. We have before us a transcendent God who *chooses* to reveal—to make comprehensible—in a manner that enabled this human being, Moses, to make some sense out of the encounter. Moses wasn't just left with vague feelings of the holy. He brought back to the people some clear, concrete understandings of God's nature and God's will, which grew out of his ability to relate to God "as one speaks to [a] friend." In these encounters God was imminent, personal, and approachable.

In the New Testament Scripture, we read that "God sent the Son into the world, not to condemn the world, but that the world might be saved through him" (John 3:17, RSV). As Christians, we confess that the clearest, truest vision of God is revealed in the Son of God, Jesus Christ. And what do we see? What is that vision? We behold a God who comes to us not to condemn but to save. We encounter love in its purest form—a love so strong that its power sustains us beyond the grave. It makes us want to take a deep breath and say, "Well, now, that's some friend!"

Those who can accept the incarnation—the notion that the nature of God is revealed in the life, death, and resurrection of Jesus Christ—are given a host of gospel images revealing the friendly face of a forgiving God. When we clear away the clutter of the centuries, we find story after story of love springing up in the most surprising places toward the least deserving people.

Jesus tells us that "there must be no limit to your goodness, as your heavenly Father's [Parent's] goodness knows no bounds" (Matthew 5:48). And, indeed, there was no limit to the goodness of Jesus Christ. His friendship knew no artificial boundaries. He called a despised tax-gatherer to be included among the intimate inner circle of disciples. He broke the religious rules to heal the sick on the sabbath, out of compassion. He ate supper with sinners, commenting that "it is not the healthy that need a doctor, but the sick" (Matthew 9:12). And, lest they miss the point, he spoke plain words: "I did not come to invite virtuous people, but sinners" (v. 13).

When the Word which was God was made flesh, who was Christ, we were given a glimpse of God through one who moved among us, who lived like us *and died* like us—a tangible, historical, concrete human being. The incarnation bridged the gap between God and humanity. When we see God in Christ, loving the world so much that God gave an only Son, we see that God has a friendly face.

If God is our friend, then what is God like? God is loving. In days like ours, when the word "love" is commonplace in soap operas, romance novels, and popular music, we risk being desensitized to its true meaning and full implications. When a pop singing group croons that love is the answer, it begins to feel like a commodity one can purchase at the nearest drug store. But the product has become so generic that we are no longer sure what it looks like.

To talk, then, in any meaningful way about the love of God, we must intentionally separate ourselves from the contemporary cacophony, and let the Scriptures speak to us afresh. Here we find God reaching out in compassion to human beings in all the conditions of life—the joy of birth, the pain of death, the invigoration of health, the depression of illness, the excitement of learning, the boredom of stagnation, the exhultation of success, the disappointment of failure, the sweetness of freedom, the outrage of injustice. God's love is *persistently present,* supporting, sustaining, nurturing, healing—no strings attached.

The friendly face of God also is dependable. God is unequivocally committed to both creatures and creation. This capacity to be counted on sometimes looks different from our desires and imaginings. If your ten-year-old decides to test God's dependability by praying for a new bicycle and then waiting to see if the prayer "works," she may be sorely disappointed. If, indeed, the bike *does* appear, the fountain of goodness undoubtedly is parental, not eternal!

The dependability of God is not subject to human manipulation. Nevertheless, God can be trusted to support and sustain us in all the vagaries of life. Our task is to discern *how* this is occurring and what it means for us at any given moment. I will always remember the television movie about Jean Donovan, the Roman Catholic lay missionary who, with three of her religious colleagues, was slain in 1980 in El Salvador. She apparently wrote in her journal about a time of loneliness, confusion, and struggle, in which she was feeling abandoned by both God and humanity. She took these feelings to God in a plaintive prayer of protest. "Remember, Lord, that day when I was walking all alone on the beach? Where were you when I needed you?" And then she knew. When only one set of footprints appeared in the sand, they belonged to God, who was cradling her in Holy arms. These were the words she used to describe her feelings of assurance. They echo the penned convictions of an anonymous writer whose brief story "Footprints" is found printed on plaques on many a wall. God's presence could be relied on. God is dependable.

The friendly face of God also is forgiving. We assert this in worship every Sunday morning, in our words of assurance following the prayer of confession, in the Lord's Prayer, in many of the hymns we sing. Yet how many of us really appropriate this magnificent gift in the core of our being? How many of us are haunted by failings, large and small, which we are afraid to expose to the grace of God? Many of us harbor a tendency to fence God into our own limited notions of forgiveness. But God's grace cannot be confined by our human expectations. God will not be hemmed in.

I was reading from the Methodist founder John Wesley's *Journal* recently, and I was struck by the timing of his formative encounter with a forgiving God. It occurred on the heels of failure. While Wesley was in Georgia on a missionary expedition, he fell in love, only to be spurned by his "intended." Wesley was so outraged by the rebuff that he excommunicated the poor girl! She, in turn, had friends in high places, who put out a warrant for Wesley's arrest. He was forced to flee the colonies, and a friend bribed a captain to gain passage for him on a ship returning to England!

Wesley obviously had a lot to think about! He said, "I went to America to convert the Indians but, oh, who shall convert me?"[2] Plagued by guilt, he described his new understanding of the forgiving nature of God as follows:

> In the evening, I went very unwillingly to a society in Aldersgate Street, where one was reading Luther's Preface to the Epistle to the Romans. About a quarter before nine, while he was describing the change which God works in the heart through faith in Christ, I felt my heart strangely warmed . . . and an assurance was given me that he had taken away *my* sins, even *mine*. . . .[3]

Wesley clearly was in need of the forgiving love of God. He struggled with his ignominious departure from Georgia. And he discovered that God's forgiveness exceeded his limited imagination. God could take away *"my* sins, even *mine."* And so it can be with us. God is forgiving far beyond our expectations, if we but ask.

Love, dependability, forgiveness—these are the qualities of the God who is our friend.

If, then, God is our friend, what difference should it make? How might it affect our lives? I can think of at least

---

[2]Frank Whaling, ed., *John and Charles Wesley: Selected Prayers, Hymns, Journal Notes, Sermons, Letters and Treaties* (New York: Paulist Press, 1981), p. 100.

[3]*Ibid.*, p. 107.

two concrete consequences. You may discover others as well.

First, if God is our friend, we will seek God out, in the same way we would our most cherished earthly companion, to share the most intimate joys, hopes, and cares in our lives. We will literally "talk to" God, daring, like Moses, to approach God "face to face, as one speaks to [a] friend." The primary ground rule for these conversations should be honesty. We should not have to pretend, to hide, to make excuses in the presence of a true friend.

We call this kind of divine/human conversation "prayer." It differs from human conversations because there is no voice, no face, at the other "end of the line." We do not get any kind of instant reply that can be verified on some tape recorder.

Instead, God answers our prayers in our struggles to comprehend and respond to those matters which move us most deeply, in ways which reflect the mind of Christ. As British Methodist Neville Ward explains, "The more trust there is, and the less struggle, the better the life of faith goes. And gradually the sense of receiving, of being given this and that, comes."[4]

What we receive is not in the "new bicycle" category. No —it comes in the form of strength, solace, support; new insights, changed perspective, firmer resolve; uneasiness, vague discontent, gentle pangs of conscience. And so we take these gifts from God our friend and incorporate them into our lives—sometimes with no immediate changes, other times with surprising shifts.

If God is our friend, we will want to spend time with God. We will take the relationship seriously. And it will have consequences.

Second, if God is our friend, we will not want to rupture the relationship. In other words, this divine-human friendship has ethi-

[4]J. Neville Ward, *The Following Plough* (London: Epworth Press, 1978), p. 27.

cal consequences. Insofar as is humanly possible, we will want to respond to God's dependability with a faithfulness of our own. We will reflect those qualities of God—love, dependability, and forgiveness—in our relationships with one another.

As Christians, our efforts to be responsible, to do our duty, to strive for fairness, to show love—all have a meaning beyond themselves. We point not only to the human consequences of these acts of goodness but also to the God our friend who provides the underlying rationale for our behavior.

One of the very public couples who illustrate this link between the dependability of God and the faithfulness of humanity is Jimmy and Rosalynn Carter. Regardless of our reactions to the Carter presidency (he clearly received mixed reviews!), I find their post–White House years intriguing. The Carters have made no secret of their Protestant piety. In fact, the very public proclamation of it made some of us squirm. When the lofty levels of delicate diplomacy were closed to the President by the fate of the ballot box, the Carters took their God-dependent sense of ethical responsibility into lowlier channels. With little fanfare (considering the President's former role as leader of this nation), they have gone into the tenements of Harlem and the slums of the Carribean, rebuilding and refurbishing homes for the poor under the auspices of a church-inspired project called Habitat for Humanity.

This behavior—remarkable in its tangibility and humility—illustrates the way in which two committed Christians are responding to the love of God through their love of human beings. If God is our friend, we will want to respond with a faithfulness and friendliness of our own.

So, there you have it—a thumbnail sketch of God as our friend: loving, dependable, forgiving, drawing us toward intimacy, sending us into the world to mirror God's love.

If a little child should come to you and ask, "What is God

like?" what will you say? Does *your* God have a friendly face? If the answer is "yes," it is bound to make a profound difference in your life.

PRAYER

Gracious God, who has lifted the veil of mystery enough to reveal Yourself as Friend, I respond in wonder and gratitude. Help me to accept Your dependable, forgiving love in ways which free me also to be dependable, forgiving, and loving. I long to live out of the assurance of Your love. In the name of Jesus Christ I pray.
Amen.

Appendix

Some Questions
for Thought and Discussion

The following questions may be used either as aids in personal reflection and meditation or as stimulants to group dialogue.

Chapter 1

How would you characterize the pace of your life? Why? Give some examples of factors that contribute to your "personal pace."

Do you face dilemmas in "friendship formation"? Describe some of them.

Have you experienced some of the "marks" of friendship, on either the giving or receiving end? What form did they take? How did they feel?

In what ways could you be a better "giver" of friendship?

Have you ever experienced the loving presence of God in friendship? What made it a "grace-filled" moment? How did it contribute to your understanding of God?

Chapter 2

How do you react when you hear Jesus' words, "I did not come to invite virtuous people, but sinners" (Matthew 9:13)? What do these words mean *for you?*

What do these words reveal about God?

What do they say about the ways we deal with each other?

What changes do you want to make in your life in light of this Good News about God's forgiving love? If these changes seem difficult, do you feel you can turn to God for help?

Chapter 3

When you hear the words "piety" and "pious," what images come to mind? Is humor ever among them?

What makes you laugh? Do any of the sources of your laughter ever humor you into humility or unmask your idolatries? In what ways?

When you hear a humorous story, do you like to share it?

Have you ever encountered a situation when humor was redemptive? How did it "save the day" or save the situation?

Can you imagine finding God through humor? If so, how does God appear?

Chapter 4

How well do you balance work and play? Is there a problem?

Do any of the three tendencies which cause people to lead imbalanced lives apply to you? Why?

When, if ever, have you experienced a connection between religion and recreation? Describe it.

Do you think it is possible to know the gracious love of God in all its fullness without including recreation in the rhythm of your life?

What would you have to change in order to experience this? How might friends fit into the mix?

Chapter 5

Were you surprised by the enumeration of conflicts in the New Testament? Did it change your perceptions about the relationships among "the saints"? In what ways? If Jesus Christ was embroiled in conflicts, what might this say about the nature of conflict? About human nature?

What was the most recent conflict you had with a friend? in your church? What was it about? Was it a "fair" fight?

In what ways might God have been present in those situations? What makes you think so?

Did reconciliation occur? How? Was forgiveness a factor?

Chapter 6

If you knew that you were going to die tomorrow, how would you spend the next twenty-four hours?

Have you ever been on the giving or the receiving end of various friendly expressions of sympathy and support which came at times of bereavement? How did the experience make you feel?

William Penn said, "We can fall no deeper than God's arms can reach, however deep we fall."[1] Have you experienced the sense of trust described by Penn? When? What difference did it make?

The apostle Paul poses the question "Then what can separate us from the love of Christ?" (Romans 8:35). How would you answer his question? How might it change your behavior toward yourself? your friends?

[1]Douglas V. Steere, *Quaker Spirituality: Selected Writings* (New York: Paulist Press, 1984), p. 237.

Chapter 7

Do you discuss experiences in your spiritual quest with a friend? If so, how and when? If not, what keeps you from doing so?

What is your understanding of the nature of Christian baptism?

Have you ever participated in a worship service during which you renewed your baptismal vows? Did the service affect your understanding of your call in any way?

How frequently, and in what ways, do you "exercise your spiritual muscles"?

If you were to take more seriously the notion of "Christian friendship," what changes would you make in your friendships? Has your faith been shaped in any ways by a friend of the soul? How, and by whom? What was it that he/she said or did which was formative for you? Have you shared the learning with anyone else?

Chapter 8

If your lifestyle were elevated to be a model of Christian behavior emulated by others, of what would you be proud? What would embarrass you?

How would you describe your church's lifestyle? How closely do your church's faith commitments correspond to your church's budget?

What was Jesus' "lifestyle"? Which of his parables illustrate his commitments most clearly for you?

If you were to make one change in your lifestyle, beginning tomorrow, what would it be? Why?

Chapter 9

If your son or daughter, niece or nephew heard the story of the good Samaritan and then asked you, "Who is *my* neighbor?" what would you say? How large a circle would you draw?

When was the last time you were faced with an issue on which you felt compelled to take a stand? Why? How did it relate to your Christian commitments?

If you were to use one word to describe the lifestyle of Americans, what would it be? How comfortable are you with your assessment? Why? In what ways might friends support one another in their efforts to be better global neighbors?

Chapter 10

If you were to draw a picture of God, what would God look like? Or if a child asked you, "What is God like?" what would you say?

Do you ever relate to God "as one speaks to [a] friend"? When? How?

Which images in the Gospels most clearly reveal the friendly face of a forgiving God to you?

If God is our friend, what difference should it make? How does this affect *your* life?